Mastering Linux

The Complete Guide for SysAdmins and Power Users Become an expert in Linux system administration and command-line efficiency

THOMPSON CARTER

Table of Content

TABLE OF CONTENTS

Introduction

Mastering Linux: The Complete Guide for SysAdmins and Power Users

Linux has become one of the most widely adopted operating systems across the globe, powering everything from personal devices to enterprise-grade servers and high-performance supercomputers. Whether you are a seasoned system administrator, a developer, or a power user looking to deepen your understanding of Linux, this book is designed to be your comprehensive guide to mastering Linux for real-world scenarios.

In this rapidly changing technological landscape, Linux's open-source nature, flexibility, and powerful performance make it the ideal choice for both personal and professional use. However, its depth and complexity require a solid understanding of its core concepts, tools, and best practices to manage and maintain Linux systems effectively. This book covers everything from the fundamental concepts that form the foundation of Linux to advanced techniques used by experts to manage large-scale, high-performance systems.

Target Audience

This book is written for a wide range of individuals who interact with Linux systems, including:

- **System Administrators (SysAdmins)**: If you are a sysadmin looking to streamline and secure your Linux servers, this book will give you the tools you need to monitor, maintain, and optimize your systems, ensuring they perform optimally and securely under heavy workloads.
- **Developers**: Whether you are developing applications for Linux or deploying software in production environments, this book will help you understand how to set up and configure your environment for success. We will cover everything from using the command line efficiently to setting up containerized applications and managing system resources.
- **Power Users**: If you are an advanced Linux user looking to enhance your skills, we will take you beyond the basics, diving deep into system

performance, security, and automation techniques that can help you work faster and more effectively with Linux.

- **Beginners**: Even if you're new to Linux, don't worry. This book offers a step-by-step guide to understanding the Linux file system, command-line operations, and essential administration tasks, making it approachable for those starting their Linux journey.

What You'll Learn

This book is organized into structured parts, each focusing on a specific aspect of Linux system administration and usage:

- **Part 1: Introduction to Linux**: We begin with the basics of Linux—what it is, its history, and why it is the operating system of choice for sysadmins and developers. You'll learn how to navigate the Linux file system, work with packages, and understand the essential tools that form the backbone of any Linux system.
- **Part 2: Linux Command Line Essentials**: As a Linux power user or sysadmin, the command line

will become your best friend. This section covers everything from basic file operations to advanced shell commands and scripting. By the end of this section, you'll have a deep understanding of how to automate repetitive tasks and work more efficiently.

- **Part 3: System Administration Fundamentals**: This section dives into the heart of system administration—user management, file permissions, package management, and process monitoring. These are core skills every sysadmin must master to ensure the security, stability, and efficiency of their systems.

- **Part 4: Networking in Linux**: Networking is a critical aspect of any modern IT environment. In this section, we cover the essentials of Linux networking, from basic configuration to advanced topics like firewall management and remote connections. You'll gain the skills necessary to manage network services securely.

- **Part 5: Linux Storage Management**: Learn how to manage disks, partitions, logical volumes, and file systems. We'll also cover disk encryption, RAID configurations, and file system performance tuning, providing you with the expertise to manage storage on Linux effectively.

- **Part 6: Security Essentials**: Security is a critical part of any system administrator's role. We'll take you through securing Linux systems, including configuring SSH access, managing user accounts, securing file systems, and using tools like SELinux and AppArmor for access control.

- **Part 7: Auditing and Compliance**: Learn how to audit your Linux systems for security breaches and compliance with regulations like GDPR. This section will cover essential auditing tools, log management, and generating reports to ensure that your Linux environment is secure and meets regulatory standards.

- **Part 8: Advanced Topics**: Finally, we explore more advanced topics such as system performance optimization, virtualization, containerization, and managing services with tools like systemd. These skills are essential for sysadmins who need to handle complex and high-demand systems.

Why This Book?

Linux is not just an operating system; it's a way of life for many IT professionals. By mastering Linux, you gain the power to automate tasks, secure systems, build scalable solutions, and leverage the full potential of modern computing. However, to harness the full power of Linux, you need more than just a surface-level understanding.

This book is designed to bridge the gap between beginner knowledge and expert-level skills. Whether you're a newbie to Linux or an experienced sysadmin, you will find invaluable insights into configuring, optimizing, and securing Linux systems. By focusing on real-world examples, hands-on exercises, and best practices, this book ensures that you're equipped to tackle any challenges you may face in a Linux environment.

Real-World Applications and Examples

The practical examples and real-world scenarios presented throughout this book provide direct relevance to the work you do daily. You'll learn how to configure a web server, secure a Linux system, set up automated backups, monitor performance, and even comply with industry regulations like GDPR.

Each chapter provides actionable steps that you can apply immediately, making this book a practical guide you can keep as a reference long after you've read it. By the end of this book, you'll be able to confidently manage Linux systems, deploy applications, and ensure that your systems remain secure, efficient, and compliant with industry standards.

Conclusion

"Mastering Linux: The Complete Guide for SysAdmins and Power Users" is your one-stop resource for mastering Linux. Whether you're just starting out or looking to deepen your expertise, this book will help you become a proficient Linux user and administrator. With its detailed coverage of essential topics, advanced techniques, and practical examples, this book ensures that you're fully prepared to handle the challenges of modern Linux environments.

Are you ready to dive into the world of Linux and unlock your system administration potential? Let's begin your journey toward mastering Linux!

Part 1

Introduction to Linux

CHAPTER 1

WHAT IS LINUX?

Linux is an open-source, Unix-like operating system that has gained widespread popularity due to its stability, flexibility, and security features. It has evolved from a small, hobbyist project into the backbone of many servers, workstations, and embedded systems around the world.

History of Linux

Linux began in 1991 when Linus Torvalds, a Finnish computer science student, released the first version of the Linux kernel. He initially wanted to create a free alternative to the proprietary operating systems available at the time, like MS-DOS and Unix. His kernel was designed to work with the GNU operating system, a collection of free software tools created by Richard Stallman and the Free Software Foundation. This union of the Linux kernel and the GNU tools resulted in a complete operating system known as GNU/Linux.

Since its inception, Linux has grown exponentially thanks to contributions from developers worldwide. Today, Linux powers a variety of devices, from web servers to smartphones, and even supercomputers.

Open-Source Philosophy

One of the core principles of Linux is its open-source nature. Open-source software is software whose source code is freely available for anyone to view, modify, and distribute. This openness encourages innovation and transparency, enabling developers to collaborate and improve the software collectively. Unlike proprietary systems like Windows or macOS, Linux's source code is accessible, meaning users can customize the OS to meet their specific needs.

The open-source community surrounding Linux is vast, with thousands of developers and organizations contributing to its development. Popular distributions (distros) like Ubuntu, Fedora, and Debian are built upon the Linux kernel but offer different tools and configurations suited for various purposes, such as desktop use, development, or server environments.

Why Linux is the Operating System for SysAdmins and Power Users

Linux has become the go-to operating system for system administrators (sysadmins) and power users for several reasons:

1. **Stability and Reliability:** Linux is known for its stability. It runs efficiently under heavy workloads and can operate continuously for long periods without requiring a reboot. This makes it a preferred choice for servers and production environments where uptime is critical.

2. **Flexibility and Customization:** Linux offers unparalleled flexibility. Sysadmins can tailor the system to their needs, from configuring the kernel to choosing different desktop environments or managing software through package managers. This level of customization is ideal for those who need to optimize their systems for specific tasks.

3. **Security:** Linux is renowned for its security features. By default, Linux has robust permissions and user management systems in place. Additionally, many distros come with built-in security tools and practices, making it a preferred choice for managing sensitive data and high-security environments.

4. **Cost-Effective:** Since Linux is open-source, it is free to use. This cost advantage is especially valuable in enterprise settings, where licensing fees for proprietary systems like Windows Server or macOS can add up quickly.

5. **Powerful Command-Line Interface (CLI):** Sysadmins and power users often prefer Linux for its powerful command-line interface. While graphical user interfaces (GUIs) are available, the CLI allows for faster, more efficient management of system resources, automation of tasks, and customization.

6. **Wide Range of Distributions:** Different Linux distributions are tailored to different needs. Some distros are focused on enterprise use, while others cater to security or multimedia production. This variety allows users to choose the best distro for their particular use case.

Real-World Example: A Comparison of Linux vs Windows in a Corporate Environment

Let's take the example of a large corporation that manages its IT infrastructure across multiple regions.

Scenario: The company has a mixed environment, with some servers running Windows Server and others running Linux-based servers (e.g., Ubuntu, CentOS).

- **Linux Servers**: These servers are used for hosting websites, databases, and email services. The company benefits from Linux's stability, security, and the low cost of ownership. Sysadmins can automate backups and maintenance tasks through scripts, and the servers run 24/7 without interruptions. Security updates are quickly deployed, and there's minimal need for resource-heavy antivirus software since Linux is inherently secure against many common types of malware.

- **Windows Servers**: On the other hand, Windows servers are used for specific business applications that require a Windows environment. However, these servers often require more frequent updates and restarts. Additionally, they tend to need more resources for antivirus software and security patches. While they are compatible with proprietary enterprise software that may not run on Linux, they are more vulnerable to external threats like viruses and ransomware, and often require more IT personnel to maintain.

Conclusion: While both operating systems have their roles in a corporate environment, Linux is the preferred choice for handling critical infrastructure, databases, and web hosting due to its stability, security, and cost-effectiveness. Windows may still be needed for certain proprietary software applications, but in the world of servers and system administration, Linux remains the go-to choice for sysadmins.

This chapter sets the stage for a deep dive into Linux, providing readers with an understanding of its history, open-source nature, and why it is favored by sysadmins and power users. The next chapter will explore how to get started with installing and configuring Linux, setting up your system for optimal use.

CHAPTER 2

INSTALLING AND SETTING UP LINUX

In this chapter, we will explore the different Linux distributions, their use cases, and the various methods for installing Linux on your system. Whether you are setting up Linux for testing, development, or production use, this chapter will guide you through the installation process with real-world examples and practical insights.

Different Linux Distributions and Their Use Cases

Linux is not just one operating system; it's a family of operating systems, each suited for specific purposes. The "distribution" or "distro" is the version of Linux that you choose to install. Different distros have various tools, user interfaces, and package management systems, but all share the same Linux kernel. Here are some of the most popular distributions and their typical use cases:

1. **Ubuntu**:
    - o **Use Case**: General-purpose, desktop computing, development, and cloud.

- o **Description**: Ubuntu is one of the most popular Linux distributions. It's user-friendly and perfect for beginners. With its broad community support and frequent updates, Ubuntu is ideal for both desktop users and developers looking to set up a development environment.

2. **CentOS (now CentOS Stream)**:
   - o **Use Case**: Servers, enterprise environments, web hosting.
   - o **Description**: CentOS is widely used for server environments due to its stability and long-term support. It's based on Red Hat Enterprise Linux (RHEL) and shares many of the same features, making it ideal for production environments. CentOS Stream is a rolling release that allows users to preview upcoming RHEL features.

3. **Debian**:
   - o **Use Case**: Servers, development, and desktop computing.
   - o **Description**: Debian is known for its stability and reliability. It is the basis for many other distros, including Ubuntu. It's commonly used in server environments and is a favorite among sysadmins due to its minimalistic approach and long-term support.

4. **Fedora**:

o **Use Case**: Desktop use, development, bleeding-edge software.

o **Description**: Fedora is known for staying on the cutting edge with the latest software and features. It is often chosen by developers who want to work with the newest Linux technologies. It serves as a testbed for RHEL, and it is well-suited for users who prefer to have the latest features.

5. **Arch Linux**:

o **Use Case**: Advanced users, custom setups.

o **Description**: Arch is a minimalistic and highly flexible Linux distribution. It's ideal for advanced users who want to build their system from the ground up. Arch provides rolling releases and does not include unnecessary software, so users have full control over their system configuration.

6. **Linux Mint**:

o **Use Case**: Desktop use, for Linux beginners.

o **Description**: Linux Mint is based on Ubuntu and is designed for ease of use. It comes with a full range of pre-installed software, making it perfect for new Linux users who want a polished desktop experience. It has a similar interface to Windows, which makes it easier for new users to transition.

7. **Raspberry Pi OS** (formerly Raspbian):

- o **Use Case**: Raspberry Pi single-board computers, DIY projects.
- o **Description**: Raspberry Pi OS is a Debian-based distribution optimized for the Raspberry Pi hardware. It's commonly used in educational settings and DIY projects, where small, low-cost computers are used to build hardware systems.

Installation Steps (Live CDs, Virtual Machines, Dual Boot)

Now that we've covered some common distributions, it's time to look at the different methods you can use to install Linux. Each method offers unique advantages depending on whether you're testing Linux, setting it up for development, or running it as your primary operating system.

1. **Live CDs/USBs**:
   - o **What It Is**: A Live CD/USB allows you to boot and run Linux directly from a CD or USB drive without installing it on your computer's hard drive. This is an excellent way to test out a Linux distribution before deciding to install it.
   - o **How to Use It**:
     - Download the ISO file of the Linux distribution you want to try.
     - Create a bootable CD or USB drive using tools like Rufus or balenaEtcher.

23

- Boot your computer from the Live CD/USB and explore Linux without making any changes to your system.

2. **Virtual Machines (VMs)**:

   o **What It Is**: A virtual machine allows you to run Linux inside your current operating system, providing an isolated environment for testing or running Linux applications. This is ideal for development or testing without modifying your primary OS.

   o **How to Set Up**:

     - Install a hypervisor like VirtualBox or VMware.
     - Create a new virtual machine and allocate resources like RAM and disk space.
     - Mount the ISO file of the Linux distribution and start the VM.
     - Follow the installation prompts to complete the Linux setup within the virtual machine.

3. **Dual Boot**:

   o **What It Is**: Dual booting allows you to install Linux alongside another operating system, such as Windows. When you start your computer, you can choose which OS to boot into.

24

- o **How to Set Up**:
  - Backup your data before beginning the dual-boot process.
  - Create a partition for Linux using a tool like GParted or Windows Disk Management.
  - Install the Linux distribution on the new partition, and the installer will configure a bootloader (like GRUB) that allows you to choose between operating systems during startup.
  - Be mindful of potential issues with bootloaders, especially when dealing with UEFI/BIOS configurations.

Real-World Example: Setting Up Ubuntu on a Virtual Machine for Testing

In this section, we'll walk through the process of setting up Ubuntu on a VirtualBox virtual machine for testing purposes. This is a common scenario for developers and sysadmins who need a safe environment to test software or commands without affecting their main system.

1. **Step 1: Download Ubuntu ISO**
   - o Go to the official Ubuntu download page and select the latest stable version.

25

o Save the ISO file to your computer.

2. **Step 2: Install VirtualBox**

o Download and install VirtualBox from VirtualBox's official website.

o After installation, open VirtualBox and click "New" to create a new VM.

3. **Step 3: Create the Virtual Machine**

o Name your VM (e.g., "Ubuntu Test").

o Select the operating system version (Ubuntu 64-bit).

o Allocate RAM (e.g., 2GB or more, depending on your system resources).

o Create a new virtual hard disk (e.g., 20GB or more, choose VDI for flexibility).

4. **Step 4: Mount the Ubuntu ISO**

o With the VM selected, click "Settings" and go to the "Storage" tab.

o Under "Controller: IDE," click the empty disk icon, then click the disk icon on the right and choose "Choose a disk file."

o Select the Ubuntu ISO you downloaded earlier.

5. **Step 5: Start the VM**

o Click "Start" to begin the installation process.

o Follow the on-screen instructions to install Ubuntu, selecting your language, keyboard layout, and user preferences.

o   Once the installation is complete, the system will ask you to restart the virtual machine.

6. **Step 6: Log in and Explore**

o   After rebooting, log in with the username and password you set during installation.

o   You can now use Ubuntu on your virtual machine, testing software, commands, or configurations without affecting your primary OS.

This chapter has covered the different ways to install Linux, with an emphasis on virtual machines for testing. Whether you're looking to test Linux on your own computer or set up a more permanent installation, this guide ensures you're prepared for the process. The next chapter will focus on navigating the Linux filesystem, which is essential for any sysadmin or power user to master.

CHAPTER 3

NAVIGATING THE LINUX FILESYSTEM

In this chapter, we will dive into the Linux filesystem. Understanding how Linux organizes its files and directories, along with how to navigate and manipulate them, is fundamental to being an effective system administrator or power user. We'll also explore how Linux handles file permissions and types to secure your system.

Filesystem Hierarchy and Directory Structure

The Linux filesystem follows a hierarchical structure, which organizes files into directories. At the top of this structure is the root directory, denoted as /. All other directories are contained within this root directory. The hierarchy is designed to keep files organized, and the structure remains consistent across different Linux distributions.

Here's an overview of the key directories in the Linux filesystem:

1. **/ (Root)**:

- o This is the top-most directory. All other directories and files reside under it.
- o Example: /home, /etc, /usr

2. /bin (Binaries):

- o Contains essential command binaries (programs) that are required for basic system functionality.
- o Example: /bin/ls for listing directory contents, /bin/bash for the shell.

3. /etc (Configuration Files):

- o Holds configuration files for system-wide settings, such as network configurations, user authentication, and software settings.
- o Example: /etc/passwd for user account information, /etc/network/interfaces for network settings.

4. /home (User Home Directories):

- o Contains personal directories for users. Each user has their own directory under /home.
- o Example: /home/john for the user "john".

5. /usr (User Programs and Data):

- o Contains user applications and data that are not required for the system to function but are essential for day-to-day use.
- o Example: /usr/bin contains additional executable programs, /usr/share holds application data.

6. **/var (Variable Files)**:
   - o Stores files that are expected to change frequently, such as logs, mail, and print spoolers.
   - o Example: `/var/log` for system logs, `/var/mail` for user mailboxes.

7. **/tmp (Temporary Files)**:
   - o A location for temporary files that are often created by applications. Files here are typically deleted upon reboot.
   - o Example: `/tmp/xyz` could be a temporary file created during installation.

8. **/lib (Libraries)**:
   - o Contains shared libraries needed by essential binaries found in `/bin` and `/sbin`.
   - o Example: `/lib/x86_64-linux-gnu/libc.so.6` for the C standard library.

9. **/dev (Devices)**:
   - o Houses files that represent hardware devices. Linux uses a file-based interface for hardware devices (e.g., disks, printers).
   - o Example: `/dev/sda` represents the first hard drive, `/dev/tty1` for terminal 1.

10. **/mnt and /media (Mount Points)**:
    - o **/mnt** is a temporary mount point for manually mounted filesystems.

o **/media** is used for automatically mounted devices such as USB drives or CDs.

o Example: /mnt/data might be where an additional disk is mounted.

11. **/opt (Optional Software)**:

o Contains third-party software packages that are not part of the core operating system.

o Example: /opt/google for Google applications.

12. **/proc (Kernel and Process Information)**:

o Contains virtual files that provide information about the system, including running processes and kernel parameters.

o Example: /proc/cpuinfo for CPU information, /proc/1 for process 1 (init).

Understanding Paths, Permissions, and File Types

- **Paths**:

  o Linux uses absolute and relative paths to specify the location of files and directories.

    ▪ **Absolute Path**: Starts from the root directory /. Example: /etc/hostname

    ▪ **Relative Path**: Starts from the current directory. Example: ./documents (refers to "documents" in the current directory).

- **Permissions**:
  - Files in Linux have permissions that dictate who can read, write, or execute the file.
  - The permissions are displayed as a string of 10 characters, for example: `-rwxr-xr--`
    - The first character represents the file type (e.g., `-` for regular files, `d` for directories).
    - The next three characters represent the owner's permissions (e.g., `rwx` means read, write, execute).
    - The next three characters represent the group's permissions.
    - The last three characters represent others' permissions.

Common Permissions:

  - **r**: Read permission allows the file to be opened and read.
  - **w**: Write permission allows modifying the file.
  - **x**: Execute permission allows running the file as a program or script.

You can modify permissions with the `chmod` command:

- `chmod 755 filename`: Gives full permissions to the owner and read/execute permissions to others.

- `chmod 644 filename`: Gives read/write permissions to the owner and read-only permissions to others.

- **File Types**:
  - Files can belong to different types, such as:
    - **Regular files**: Represent documents, programs, or scripts.
    - **Directories**: Folders that hold other files or directories.
    - **Symbolic links**: Shortcuts that point to other files or directories.
    - **Block and character devices**: Represent hardware devices, such as hard drives or terminals.
    - **Sockets and pipes**: Used for inter-process communication.

Real-World Example: Finding a Configuration File on a Server

In a production environment, you may need to find a specific configuration file on a Linux server, such as a web server's configuration for Apache.

Here's how to do it:

1. **Step 1: Use `find` to Search for the File**
   o If you're not sure where the configuration file is located, you can use the `find` command to search for it. For example:

   bash

   ```
   sudo find / -name "apache2.conf"
   ```

   o This command will search from the root directory `/` for a file named `apache2.conf`. The `sudo` is used because configuration files are often stored in protected directories that require root access.

2. **Step 2: Check Common Directories**
   o Most configuration files are stored in the `/etc` directory. So, you can also check directly in `/etc`:

   bash

34

```
ls /etc | grep apache2
```

o   This command lists all files in /etc and filters
    them for those related to Apache.

3. **Step 3: Inspect the File**

    o   Once you've located the file, you can use a text
        editor like nano or vim to view and edit it:

    ```
    bash
    ```

    ```
    sudo nano /etc/apache2/apache2.conf
    ```

    o   This will open the apache2.conf file in the
        nano text editor, where you can make changes to
        the web server's configuration.

4. **Step 4: Verify Changes**

    o   After making changes to configuration files, it's
        important to verify them before restarting
        services:

    ```
    bash
    ```

    ```
    sudo apache2ctl configtest
    ```

    o   This command checks the configuration for any
        syntax errors. If everything is correct, you can
        safely restart Apache:

```bash

sudo systemctl restart apache2
```

This example shows how to locate and modify configuration files on a Linux server, a common task for system administrators.

In this chapter, we've covered the Linux filesystem hierarchy, how to navigate and understand paths, file permissions, and file types. By mastering this foundational knowledge, you will be able to effectively interact with files, configure systems, and manage permissions on a Linux server. In the next chapter, we'll explore how to manage users and groups, an essential skill for system administrators.

Part 2

Linux Command Line Essentials

CHAPTER 4: BASIC COMMAND-LINE SKILLS

The command line is the heart of Linux system administration. Whether you're a sysadmin or a power user, mastering basic shell commands will greatly enhance your productivity. In this chapter, we will cover essential commands for navigating directories, performing file operations, and using the Linux shell effectively. These foundational skills are crucial for anyone working in a Linux environment.

Navigating Directories

One of the first steps in using the command line is navigating the filesystem. Linux uses a hierarchical directory structure, and understanding how to move through this structure efficiently is key to being productive.

1. **pwd (Print Working Directory)**:
   - This command shows the current directory you are working in.
   - Example:

   ```
   bash
   ```

```
$ pwd
/home/user
```

- o   This tells you that you are currently in the /home/user directory.

2. **cd (Change Directory)**:
   - o   Use cd to change to a different directory.
   - o   Example:

   bash

   ```
   $ cd /etc
   ```

   - o   This changes the current directory to /etc. You can also use relative paths:

   bash

   ```
   $ cd ../
   ```

   - o   This moves you up one level in the directory hierarchy.

3. **ls (List Directory Contents)**:
   - o   This command lists the contents of a directory.
   - o   Example:

   bash

   ```
   $ ls
   ```

```
Desktop    Documents    Downloads
```

o   To see detailed information about the files (e.g., permissions, sizes), use -l (long format):

```
bash
```

```
$ ls -l
```

4. cd ~ (Home Directory):

o   The tilde ~ represents the home directory of the current user. Using cd ~ quickly takes you to your home directory.

o   Example:

```
bash
```

```
$ cd ~
$ pwd
/home/user
```

File Operations

Linux provides a set of commands to manage files and directories, allowing you to create, move, rename, , and delete files.

1. touch (Create a File):

40

- o Use `touch` to create an empty file or update the timestamp of an existing file.
- o Example:

```bash

$ touch example.txt
```

2. cp (Files):

- o Use `cp` to files or directories from one location to another.
- o Example:

```bash

$          cp          example.txt
/home/user/Documents/
```

3. mv (Move or Rename Files):

- o Use `mv` to move or rename files and directories.
- o Example (renaming a file):

```bash

$ mv example.txt example_renamed.txt
```

- o Example (moving a file to another directory):

```bash

```

41

```
$        mv        example_renamed.txt
/home/user/Documents/
```

4. rm (Remove Files):

o   Use rm to remove files.

o   Example:

```
bash
```

```
$ rm example_renamed.txt
```

5. rmdir (Remove Empty Directories):

o   Use rmdir to remove empty directories.

o   Example:

```
bash
```

```
$ rmdir empty_directory
```

6. rm -r (Remove Non-Empty Directories):

o   If the directory contains files, use -r (recursive) to remove the directory and all of its contents.

o   Example:

```
bash
```

```
$ rm -r directory_to_remove
```

7. **cat (Concatenate and Display Files)**:

   o Use cat to display the contents of a file on the terminal.

   o Example:

   bash

   ```
   $ cat example.txt
   ```

8. **man (Manual Pages)**:

   o Use man to display the manual for a command. This is invaluable for learning more about the available options for each command.

   o Example:

   bash

   ```
   $ man ls
   ```

Basic Shell Commands

Linux provides a powerful shell that enables you to automate tasks, create scripts, and perform complex operations efficiently. In addition to the file management commands covered above, here are a few basic shell commands that every user should know:

1. **echo (Print to the Terminal)**:

43

- o Use echo to display a message or variable value in the terminal.
- o Example:

```bash

$ echo "Hello, world!"
Hello, world!
```

2. clear (Clear the Terminal Screen):

- o Use clear to clear the terminal screen of previous commands and output.
- o Example:

```bash

$ clear
```

3. exit (Exit the Shell):

- o Use exit to exit the current shell session.
- o Example:

```bash

$ exit
```

4. history (Command History):

o Use `history` to view a list of previously executed commands. You can also reuse commands from the history.

o Example:

```bash

$ history
1  ls
2  cd Documents
3  mkdir new_folder
```

o To execute a command from history, type `!` followed by the command number:

```bash

$ !2
```

5. `find` (Search for Files):

o Use `find` to search for files in a directory based on specific criteria.

o Example:

```bash

$ find /home/user -name "*.txt"
```

o   This will search for all `.txt` files in the `/home/user` directory.

Real-World Example: Managing Files and Folders for a Simple Web Application

Let's take a practical example of managing files and folders for a simple web application using basic command-line skills.

Imagine you are deploying a simple Node.js application on a server. The project includes several files such as the `index.html`, `app.js`, and a `config.json` file. You will need to manage these files and directories using the command line.

1. **Step 1: Organize the Project Files** First, create the necessary directories for your project:

    ```bash
    $ mkdir /var/www/myapp
    $ cd /var/www/myapp
    ```

2. **Step 2: Create and Add Files** Next, create the `index.html` and `app.js` files for the application:

```
bash
```

```
$ touch index.html app.js config.json
```

3. **Step 3: Configuration Files** If you have a pre-existing `config.json` file in another directory, you can it to the project directory:

```
bash
```

```
$       cp         /home/user/config.json
/var/www/myapp/
```

4. **Step 4: Edit Files** Now, use a text editor like `nano` or `vim` to edit the files:

```
bash
```

```
$ nano app.js
```

After making changes, save and close the file.

5. **Step 5: View Files** To verify that the files were created correctly, use the `ls` command:

```
bash
```

```
$ ls
index.html  app.js  config.json
```

47

6. **Step 6: Remove Old Files** If you need to delete any unnecessary files or directories, use rm or rm -r:

bash

```
$ rm old_file.txt
$ rm -r old_directory
```

7. **Step 7: Backup Files** For backup purposes, you might want to the entire project directory to another location:

bash

```
$ cp -r /var/www/myapp /home/user/backups/
```

This chapter has covered essential Linux command-line skills for navigating directories, managing files, and using basic shell commands. With these skills, you can efficiently organize and maintain files in any Linux environment. The next chapter will dive deeper into advanced shell commands, scripting, and automation.

CHAPTER 5

ADVANCED SHELL COMMANDS

In this chapter, we will explore some advanced shell commands and techniques that will significantly improve your efficiency in Linux. Understanding concepts such as piping, redirection, and regular expressions is crucial for anyone looking to automate tasks and process data on the command line. We'll also provide a real-world example of using powerful commands like `awk`, `sed`, and `grep` to automate server log parsing.

Piping and Redirection

Linux shell provides powerful mechanisms like **piping** and **redirection** to manage the flow of data between commands. These techniques allow you to chain multiple commands together and control where the output is sent.

1. **Piping (|):**
    - Piping allows the output of one command to be passed as input to another command.
    - Example:

      ```bash
      ```

```
$ ls -l | less
```

- o In this example, ls -l lists the files in the current directory with detailed information, and | less sends the output to the less command, allowing you to scroll through the output.

2. **Redirection (> and >>):**

- o **Standard Output Redirection (>):** Redirects the output of a command to a file, overwriting the file if it already exists.

    - Example:

      bash

      ```
      $ echo "Hello, Linux!" > hello.txt
      ```

      - This command creates (or overwrites) the file hello.txt and writes "Hello, Linux!" to it.

- o **Append Redirection (>>):** Appends output to an existing file rather than overwriting it.

    - Example:

      bash

```
$ echo "Additional text" >>
hello.txt
```

- This appends "Additional text" to the end of `hello.txt` without modifying its existing content.

3. **Standard Error Redirection (2>)**:
   o Redirects error messages (stderr) to a file.
   o Example:

   ```
   bash
   ```

   ```
   $ ls non_existent_directory 2>
   error.log
   ```

   o This redirects the error message generated by trying to list a non-existent directory into the `error.log` file.

4. **Combining Output and Error Redirection (&>)**:
   o Redirects both standard output and standard error to the same file.
   o Example:

   ```
   bash
   ```

   ```
   $ ls /non_existent_dir &> output.log
   ```

51

Regular Expressions

Regular expressions (regex) are patterns used to match character combinations in strings. They are incredibly useful for searching and manipulating text in files, logs, and command outputs.

1. **Basic Syntax**:
   - o . **(dot)**: Matches any single character except a newline.
   - o * **(asterisk)**: Matches zero or more occurrences of the previous character or group.
   - o [] **(square brackets)**: Matches any single character within the brackets.
   - o ^: Anchors the match to the start of the string.
   - o $: Anchors the match to the end of the string.

   Example:

   ```bash
   $ echo "hello world" | grep "h.llo"
   ```

   - o This command searches for any word starting with 'h' and ending with 'llo' with any character in between.

2. **Using grep with Regex**:

o `grep` is the most common command for searching with regular expressions.

o Example:

```
bash
```

```
$ grep "^Error" logfile.txt
```

- This will match all lines in `logfile.txt` that start with the word "Error."

3. **Using `sed` with Regex**:

o `sed` is a stream editor for filtering and transforming text.

o Example:

```
bash
```

```
$ echo "User: john" | sed 's/john/Jane/'
```

- This command replaces "john" with "Jane" in the string "User: john".

Real-World Example: Automating Server Log Parsing with `awk,` *`sed,` and* `grep`

Managing logs is a vital task for system administrators. Logs often contain valuable information that needs to be parsed and filtered for analysis or troubleshooting. In this example, we'll automate the process of parsing server logs using `awk`, `sed`, and `grep`.

Imagine you are a sysadmin managing a web server. The server's access logs are stored in `/var/log/apache2/access.log`, and you want to:

1. **Filter logs for HTTP errors (e.g., 404 errors)**.
2. **Extract specific fields, such as IP addresses and timestamps**.
3. **Format the output into a clean report**.

Let's break down how to achieve this with the help of advanced shell commands.

Step 1: Filtering Logs for HTTP Errors

First, use `grep` to find all 404 errors in the Apache access log. HTTP 404 errors indicate that a requested resource was not found.

```
bash
```

```
$ grep " 404 " /var/log/apache2/access.log
```

This command filters the log file for any entries that contain "404". However, we want to make the output more structured.

Step 2: Extracting Specific Fields (Using `awk`)

Next, use `awk` to extract specific fields from the log file. Apache logs are typically structured with the following format:

```
swift
```

```
127.0.0.1 - - [10/Mar/2025:14:35:12 -0700] "GET
/nonexistentpage.html HTTP/1.1" 404 567 "-"
```

Here's how to use `awk` to extract the IP address and timestamp:

```
bash
```

```
$ grep " 404 " /var/log/apache2/access.log | awk
'{print $1, $4, $5, $9}'
```

- `$1` refers to the IP address.

- $4 and $5 refer to the timestamp (the square brackets with the date).
- $9 refers to the HTTP status code.

Output:

css

```
127.0.0.1 [10/Mar/2025:14:35:12 -0700] 404
```
Step 3: Formatting the Output (Using sed)

Finally, use sed to clean up and format the timestamp for easier reading. We can remove the square brackets around the timestamp and split the date from the time:

bash

```
$ grep " 404 " /var/log/apache2/access.log | awk
'{print $1, $4, $5, $9}' | sed 's/\[//g' | sed
's/\]//g' | sed 's/:/ /2'
```

- The first sed removes the opening square bracket.
- The second sed removes the closing square bracket.
- The third sed splits the date and time by replacing the first colon with a space.

Output:

```
swift
```

```
127.0.0.1 10/Mar/2025 14:35:12 404
```

Step 4: Redirecting the Output to a Report

Now that we have filtered, extracted, and formatted the log entries, let's redirect the output to a file for reporting purposes:

```
bash
```

```
$ grep " 404 " /var/log/apache2/access.log | awk
'{print $1, $4, $5, $9}' | sed 's/\[//g' | sed
's/\]//g'      |      sed     's/:/    /2'     >
/home/user/404_report.txt
```

This will save the report of 404 errors to /home/user/404_report.txt.

Summary

In this chapter, we have explored advanced shell commands like piping, redirection, and regular expressions, which are invaluable for automating tasks, searching, and manipulating text. We also provided a real-world example where these techniques were used to automate the process of parsing and filtering server logs. Mastering these commands will enable you to handle a wide variety of tasks more efficiently and automate repetitive processes in Linux.

In the next chapter, we will look into shell scripting for automation, building on the concepts we've learned so far.

CHAPTER 6

WORKING WITH TEXT FILES

In this chapter, we will cover how to work with text files in Linux, focusing on tools like `nano`, `vim`, and other command-line editors. Text files are integral to configuring and managing systems, as configuration files, logs, and scripts are typically stored in plain text format. Learning how to efficiently view, edit, and create text files is a crucial skill for any Linux user or system administrator.

Viewing Text Files

Before editing, sometimes you just need to view the contents of a text file. Linux offers a range of commands for this purpose.

1. **`cat` (Concatenate and Display Files)**:
   o The `cat` command displays the entire contents of a file.
   o Example:

   ```bash

   $ cat example.txt
   ```

o   If the file is long, this can overwhelm your terminal, so it's better suited for small files or quick inspection.

2. **`less` (View Files One Page at a Time)**:

o   The `less` command is a pager tool that allows you to view long files page-by-page.

o   Example:

```bash
$ less example.txt
```

o   You can scroll through the file using the arrow keys or `Page Up`/`Page Down`, and exit with `q`.

3. **`more` (Another Pager Tool)**:

o   The `more` command is another tool for viewing large files. It's similar to `less`, but less feature-rich.

o   Example:

```bash
$ more example.txt
```

4. **`head` and `tail` (View File's Start or End)**:

o   Use `head` to display the first few lines of a file and `tail` to view the last few lines.

o   Example:

```
bash


$ head example.txt
$ tail example.txt
```

o   You can also specify how many lines to display. For example:

```
bash


$ tail -n 20 example.txt
```

This will display the last 20 lines of the file.

5. **grep (Search Inside Files)**:

o   Use `grep` to search for specific patterns or keywords inside a file.

o   Example:

```
bash


$ grep "error" example.txt
```

o   This will search for the word "error" inside `example.txt` and show the matching lines.

Editing Text Files

Linux offers powerful text editors that allow you to modify text files directly from the command line. Two of the most commonly used editors are `nano` and `vim`.

1. **`nano` (Simple Text Editor)**:
   - `nano` is a straightforward and user-friendly text editor. It's ideal for beginners or when you need to quickly make edits to a file.
   - Example:

     bash

     ```
     $ nano example.txt
     ```

   - Once in `nano`, you can use the arrow keys to navigate, make changes, and then save the file with `Ctrl + O` and exit with `Ctrl + X`.
   - `nano` also displays helpful commands at the bottom of the screen (e.g., `Ctrl + K` to cut, `Ctrl + U` to paste).

2. **`vim` (Powerful Text Editor)**:
   - `vim` is a more advanced, feature-rich text editor that offers extensive control over text manipulation. It is the preferred choice for users

who need to perform complex edits and scripting in files.

o   Example:

```
bash


$ vim example.txt
```

o   When you open a file in `vim`, you start in **Normal Mode**, where you can navigate the file, delete text, and perform searches. To make edits, switch to **Insert Mode** by pressing `i`. After editing, press `Esc` to return to Normal Mode, then save the file with `:w` and exit with `:q`.

o   Example commands:

   ▪ To delete a line: `dd`

   ▪ To search for a word: `/word`

   ▪ To undo a change: `u`

   ▪ To redo a change: `Ctrl + r`

3. **Other Editors**:

o   **vi**: The predecessor of `vim`, often available on most Unix-like systems.

o   **emacs**: Another powerful editor with a steep learning curve, popular with certain Linux users.

o   **gedit**: A graphical text editor for GNOME-based environments, if you prefer working with a GUI.

Creating Text Files

Creating new text files in Linux can be done in various ways. Below are some common methods:

1. **Using `touch` to Create an Empty File**:
   o The `touch` command creates an empty text file if it doesn't already exist.
   o Example:

   bash

   ```
   $ touch newfile.txt
   ```

   o You can then open the file with `nano` or `vim` to add content.

2. **Using `echo` to Create and Add Content to a File**:
   o You can use `echo` to create a new file with a line of text.
   o Example:

   bash

   ```
   $ echo "Hello, World!" > newfile.txt
   ```

   o This command will create `newfile.txt` and write "Hello, World!" into it. You can use >> to append content rather than overwriting it.

3. **Using `cat` to Create a File**:

    o   `cat` can also be used to create and populate a file directly from the terminal.

    o   Example:

```bash
$ cat > newfile.txt
Hello, this is a new text file.
(Press Ctrl + D to save and exit)
```

    o   After typing the content, pressing `Ctrl + D` will save the file and return to the command prompt.

Real-World Example: Editing Configuration Files on a Live Server

Let's imagine that you're managing a web server and need to edit the configuration file for **Apache** (`httpd.conf`) or **Nginx** (`nginx.conf`) on a live server. This is a common task for sysadmins who need to adjust web server settings.

1. **Step 1: Access the Server via SSH** First, connect to the server using SSH:

```bash
$ ssh user@your-server-ip
```

65

2. **Step 2: Locate the Configuration File** Apache's configuration file might be located in `/etc/apache2/apache2.conf` or `/etc/httpd/httpd.conf`, while Nginx's configuration file is typically at `/etc/nginx/nginx.conf`. Use `nano` or `vim` to open the file:

bash

```
$ sudo nano /etc/apache2/apache2.conf
```

3. **Step 3: Make Necessary Edits** You can now edit the file as required. For example, if you want to change the `ServerAdmin` email address in the Apache configuration:

bash

```
ServerAdmin admin@example.com
```

After making your changes, save the file (`Ctrl + O` in `nano` or `:w` in `vim`).

4. **Step 4: Test the Configuration File** Before applying changes, it's a good idea to test the configuration file for errors. For Apache:

66

```
bash
```

```
$ sudo apachectl configtest
```

For Nginx:

```
bash
```

```
$ sudo nginx -t
```

5. **Step 5: Restart the Web Server** Once the configuration file is updated and tested, restart the web server to apply the changes:

   o   For Apache:

   ```
   bash
   ```

   ```
   $ sudo systemctl restart apache2
   ```

   o   For Nginx:

   ```
   bash
   ```

   ```
   $ sudo systemctl restart nginx
   ```

6. **Step 6: Verify the Changes** You can verify that the changes have taken effect by checking the web server's status:

```
bash
```

```
$ sudo systemctl status apache2
```

Or by accessing your web server through a browser to see if the new configuration is working.

Summary

In this chapter, we've explored how to view, edit, and create text files in Linux using tools like nano and vim. These tools are indispensable for system administrators who frequently work with configuration files and scripts. We also provided a real-world example of editing a web server's configuration file on a live server. Mastering these commands will improve your efficiency in managing and troubleshooting Linux systems. In the next chapter, we will explore more advanced file management techniques and automation tools that can help streamline system administration tasks.

CHAPTER 7

SHELL SCRIPTING FOR AUTOMATION

In this chapter, we will introduce the basics of shell scripting in Linux. Shell scripting allows you to automate repetitive tasks, making system administration more efficient. We'll cover how to write simple bash scripts and dive into a real-world example of automating server backups and log rotation using scripts.

Basics of Writing Bash Scripts

Bash (Bourne Again Shell) is the most commonly used shell in Linux, and it provides a powerful scripting environment. Shell scripts allow you to combine multiple commands into a single file, which can then be executed as a program. Here are the basics of writing bash scripts:

1. **Creating a Shell Script File**:
    - o To create a bash script, you simply need to create a file with a `.sh` extension (though it's not strictly necessary). You can use any text editor, such as `nano` or `vim`, to create the script.
    - o Example:

```
bash
```

```
$ nano myscript.sh
```

2. **Shebang (#!/bin/bash)**:
   - o Every bash script should start with a shebang (#!), followed by the path to the bash interpreter. This tells the system which program should be used to execute the script.
   - o Example:

```
bash
```

```
#!/bin/bash
```

3. **Making the Script Executable**:
   - o After creating your script, you need to make it executable using the chmod command.
   - o Example:

```
bash
```

```
$ chmod +x myscript.sh
```

4. **Writing Commands in the Script**:
   - o Inside the script, you can write a series of shell commands that you would typically run in the

terminal. The commands are executed in sequence when the script is run.

o Example:

```bash

#!/bin/bash
echo "Hello, World!"
```

5. **Running the Script**:

o Once the script is made executable, you can run it using ./ followed by the script name.

o Example:

```bash

$ ./myscript.sh
```

o If you get a "command not found" error, make sure the script is executable and in the current directory.

6. **Variables**:

o You can define variables in a script to store values and use them later. Variables in bash do not require a data type declaration.

o Example:

```bash

```

```
#!/bin/bash
my_var="Hello"
echo $my_var
```

7. Conditional Statements:

- o You can use if, else, and elif to create conditional statements.
- o Example:

```
bash
```

```
#!/bin/bash
if [ -f /path/to/file ]; then
    echo "File exists"
else
    echo "File does not exist"
fi
```

8. Loops:

- o You can use loops like for, while, and until to repeat commands.
- o Example (for loop):

```
bash
```

```
#!/bin/bash
for i in {1..5}
do
```

```
        echo "Iteration $i"
    done
```

9. **Functions**:

   o   Functions allow you to group commands together
       and call them as needed in your script.

   o   Example:

```
bash
```

```bash
#!/bin/bash
my_function() {
    echo "This is my function"
}
my_function
```

Real-World Example: Automating Backups and Log Rotation

One of the most common tasks for system administrators is automating backups and log rotation. Shell scripts are ideal for automating these tasks, ensuring that critical data is regularly backed up and that logs are rotated to avoid filling up disk space. Let's break down how we can automate both of these processes.

Step 1: Automating Backups

Imagine you want to back up a specific directory (e.g., /home/user/data) to an external drive or remote server every day. We'll write a bash script to perform the backup.

1. **Create the Backup Script**:
   - Open a new script file using nano:

   bash

   ```
   $ nano backup.sh
   ```

2. **Write the Script**:
   - Here is a simple script to back up the /home/user/data directory to a backup directory /backup:

   bash

   ```
   #!/bin/bash
   # Backup directory
   SOURCE_DIR="/home/user/data"
   BACKUP_DIR="/backup"
   DATE=$(date +%Y-%m-%d)
   BACKUP_FILE="$BACKUP_DIR/backup-
   $DATE.tar.gz"
   ```

74

```
# Create a backup
echo "Creating backup..."
tar -czf $BACKUP_FILE $SOURCE_DIR

# Log the backup
echo    "Backup    of    $SOURCE_DIR
completed    on    $DATE"    >>
/var/log/backup.log
```

o **Explanation**:

- We use the `tar` command to create a compressed archive of the source directory (`/home/user/data`).
- The backup file is named with the current date, using the `date` command.
- The script logs a message indicating the backup was successful, appending it to `/var/log/backup.log`.

3. **Make the Script Executable**:

```bash

$ chmod +x backup.sh
```

4. **Run the Script**:

```bash

```

75

```
$ ./backup.sh
```

5. **Schedule the Backup Using Cron**: To automate the backup on a daily basis, you can use `cron`, the job scheduler.

   o   Edit the crontab file:

   bash

   ```
   $ crontab -e
   ```

   o   Add a line to schedule the backup script to run daily at 2 AM:

   bash

   ```
   0 2 * * * /path/to/backup.sh
   ```

Step 2: Automating Log Rotation

Logs can quickly accumulate and take up disk space. We can write a script to rotate the logs, archiving old logs and keeping the most recent ones.

1. **Create the Log Rotation Script**:

   o   Open a new script file:

   bash

```
$ nano log_rotate.sh
```

2. **Write the Script**:

   o Here is a simple log rotation script that moves the current log to an archive and creates a new log file.

   bash

   ```bash
   #!/bin/bash
   # Log file path
   LOG_FILE="/var/log/myapp.log"
   ARCHIVE_DIR="/var/log/archive"
   DATE=$(date +%Y-%m-%d)

   # Rotate the log
   mv $LOG_FILE $ARCHIVE_DIR/myapp-$DATE.log

   # Create a new empty log file
   touch $LOG_FILE

   # Set appropriate permissions
   chmod 644 $LOG_FILE
   ```

   o **Explanation**:
      ▪ The script moves the current log file (myapp.log) to an archive folder with a timestamp.

77

- It then creates a new, empty log file (myapp.log).
- The chmod 644 command ensures the correct permissions are set for the new log file.

3. **Make the Script Executable**:

bash

```
$ chmod +x log_rotate.sh
```

4. **Run the Script**:

bash

```
$ ./log_rotate.sh
```

5. **Schedule the Log Rotation Using Cron**: You can also automate the log rotation by adding it to cron. For example, to rotate logs weekly:

   o Edit the crontab file:

   bash

   ```
   $ crontab -e
   ```

   o Add a line to rotate logs every Sunday at midnight:

```
bash

0 0 * * 0 /path/to/log_rotate.sh
```

Summary

In this chapter, we've learned the basics of writing bash scripts to automate tasks on Linux. We covered creating simple scripts, using variables, conditional statements, loops, and functions. We also walked through two real-world examples of automating server backups and log rotation, which are common tasks for system administrators. By mastering shell scripting, you can automate many aspects of system maintenance, improving efficiency and reducing the chance of human error.

In the next chapter, we will explore advanced shell scripting techniques, including working with user inputs, error handling, and creating more complex automation workflows.

CHAPTER 8

USER AND GROUP MANAGEMENT

Managing users and groups is an essential part of system administration in Linux. Properly configuring users and groups ensures that resources are shared securely and efficiently across different users and processes. In this chapter, we will cover how to create users, assign them to groups, and manage file permissions to control access. We'll also explore a real-world example of setting up users for a multi-developer web server.

Creating Users

In Linux, each user is identified by a unique user ID (UID) and is associated with a home directory and a shell. To create a new user, you can use the `useradd` command. By default, the `useradd` command creates a user without a password, so you'll need to set one afterward.

1. **Creating a User**:
   o   Example:

   bash

```
$ sudo useradd john
```

o This creates a user named `john`. The home directory `/home/john` will be created automatically, and the default shell (`/bin/bash`) will be assigned.

2. **Setting a Password for the User**:

   o After creating the user, set a password using the `passwd` command:

   bash

   ```
   $ sudo passwd john
   ```

   o You'll be prompted to enter and confirm the new password for the user `john`.

3. **Specifying a User's Home Directory**:

   o You can specify a custom home directory for the user when creating the user:

   bash

   ```
   $ sudo useradd -m -d /home/custom/john john
   ```

o The -m flag creates the home directory if it doesn't exist, and the -d flag allows you to specify the directory.

4. **Assigning a User to a Specific Shell**:

o By default, users are assigned the bash shell (/bin/bash). If you want to assign a different shell, you can use the -s flag:

```bash
$ sudo useradd -s /bin/zsh john
```

5. **Viewing User Information**:

o To view information about a user, you can use the id command:

```bash
$ id john
```

Creating Groups

Groups are used to organize users with similar access requirements. Groups simplify the management of permissions because you can assign permissions to a group, rather than to individual users.

1. **Creating a Group**:

o   To create a group, use the `groupadd` command:

bash

```
$ sudo groupadd developers
```

2. **Assigning Users to Groups**:

o   To add an existing user to a group, use the `usermod` command:

bash

```
$ sudo usermod -aG developers john
```

o   The `-aG` flag adds the user `john` to the `developers` group without removing them from any existing groups.

3. **Viewing Group Information**:

o   To see which groups a user belongs to, use the `groups` command:

bash

```
$ groups john
```

o   This will show all the groups that `john` is a member of.

Managing Permissions

File permissions control who can read, write, and execute files. In Linux, permissions are defined for three types of users: the file owner, the group, and others. Each file has a set of permissions represented by three characters: r (read), w (write), and x (execute).

1. **Viewing Permissions**:
   - You can use the ls -l command to view file permissions:

   ```bash
   $ ls -l /path/to/file
   ```

   - Example output:

   ```bash
   -rwxr-xr-- 1 john developers 4096 Mar 10 10:00 example.txt
   ```

     - The first character (-) indicates it's a regular file.
     - The next three characters (rwx) show that the owner (john) has read, write, and execute permissions.

84

- The next three characters (r-x) show that the group (developers) has read and execute permissions.
- The last three characters (r--) show that others have read-only permissions.

2. **Changing Permissions**:

   o Use the chmod command to change permissions.

   - To give the owner write permission:

   bash

   ```
   $ sudo chmod u+w example.txt
   ```

   - To remove write permission from others:

   bash

   ```
   $ sudo chmod o-w example.txt
   ```

3. **Changing Ownership**:

   o Use the chown command to change the owner or group of a file:

   bash

   ```
   $ sudo chown john:developers example.txt
   ```

o   This changes the ownership of `example.txt` to `john` and the group to `developers`.

4. **Setting Special Permissions (Setuid, Setgid, Sticky Bit)**:

   o   **Setuid**: Allows a user to execute a file with the permissions of the file owner.

   o   **Setgid**: Allows a user to execute a file with the permissions of the group.

   o   **Sticky Bit**: Ensures that only the file's owner can delete or rename the file in a shared directory (commonly used in `/tmp`).

Example of setting the setuid permission:

```bash

$ sudo chmod u+s /path/to/executable
```

Real-World Example: Setting Up Users for a Multi-Developer Web Server

Suppose you are setting up a web server for multiple developers working on a web application. You need to create user accounts, assign them to groups, and manage file permissions to ensure that each developer has the right level of access.

Step 1: Create User Accounts for Each Developer

Let's say you have three developers: `alice`, `bob`, and `charlie`. You will create individual user accounts for each of them.

bash

```
$ sudo useradd -m -s /bin/bash alice
$ sudo useradd -m -s /bin/bash bob
$ sudo useradd -m -s /bin/bash charlie
```

Step 2: Create a Developer Group

You want all developers to have common access to the project files, so create a group called `devs`.

bash

```
$ sudo groupadd devs
```

Step 3: Add Developers to the Group

Add each developer to the `devs` group:

bash

```
$ sudo usermod -aG devs alice
$ sudo usermod -aG devs bob
$ sudo usermod -aG devs charlie
```

Step 4: Set Up a Shared Project Directory

Create a directory where all developers will work together. You'll set the group ownership of the directory to `devs` and assign appropriate permissions.

bash

```
$ sudo mkdir /var/www/myapp
$ sudo chown :devs /var/www/myapp
$ sudo chmod 770 /var/www/myapp
```

- `770` gives read, write, and execute permissions to the owner and group, but no permissions to others.

Step 5: Grant Individual File Permissions

For files within the project directory, you may want to give each developer specific permissions. For example, if `bob` is the lead developer and should have full control over certain files, you could do:

bash

```
$         sudo         chown         bob:devs
/var/www/myapp/important_file.txt
$         sudo         chmod         770
/var/www/myapp/important_file.txt
```

Step 6: Test the Setup

You can now test the setup by logging in as different users (e.g., using `su` or `sudo` to switch users) and verifying that the permissions and group access work as expected. Each developer should be able to access the files in `/var/www/myapp`, but permissions on certain files or directories can be customized based on their role.

Summary

In this chapter, we've learned how to manage users and groups in Linux. We covered creating user accounts, assigning users to groups, and managing file permissions. We also provided a real-world example of setting up users for a multi-developer web server, ensuring that each developer has appropriate access to shared project files. Mastering user and group management is essential for maintaining a secure and organized Linux environment. In the next chapter, we'll explore more advanced system administration tasks like package management and process monitoring.

CHAPTER 9

FILE PERMISSIONS AND OWNERSHIP

In Linux, file permissions and ownership are critical for maintaining the security and integrity of the system. Understanding how to manage permissions is essential for protecting files, ensuring that only authorized users can access or modify them. In this chapter, we will dive deep into the concepts of file permissions and ownership, how to manage them, and their role in securing your system. We will also look at a real-world example of securing web application files with proper permissions.

Understanding Read, Write, and Execute Permissions

Each file and directory in Linux has permissions associated with it that dictate who can read, write, or execute it. These permissions are set for three types of users:

- **Owner**: The user who owns the file.
- **Group**: Users who are members of the file's group.
- **Others**: All other users who are not the owner or part of the group.

Each of these user categories has three basic types of permissions:

1. **Read (r)**: Allows the user to view the contents of the file or list the contents of a directory.
2. **Write (w)**: Allows the user to modify the file or add/remove files from a directory.
3. **Execute (x)**: Allows the user to run the file as a program or script. For directories, execute permission allows the user to enter (cd into) the directory and access files within it.

The permissions are represented in a string of 10 characters, like so:

```
diff
```

```
-rwxr-xr--
```

The string is broken down into three groups:

- **First character**: Type of file (- for regular file, d for directory, l for symbolic link).
- **Next three characters**: Permissions for the owner.
- **Next three characters**: Permissions for the group.
- **Last three characters**: Permissions for others.

For example:

```
diff
```

```
-rwxr-xr--
```

- The owner (rwx) has read, write, and execute permissions.
- The group (r-x) has read and execute permissions, but cannot write to the file.
- Others (r--) have only read permissions.

Changing Permissions with chmod

The chmod (change mode) command is used to modify file permissions. You can change permissions using either symbolic or numeric (octal) representation.

1. **Symbolic Representation**:
   o You can modify permissions using the r, w, and x symbols.
   o Example: Add execute permission for the owner:

   ```bash
   $ sudo chmod u+x file.txt
   ```

   o Example: Remove write permission for the group:

```
bash
```

```
$ sudo chmod g-w file.txt
```

o   Example: Give read and execute permissions to others:

```
bash
```

```
$ sudo chmod o+rx file.txt
```

2. **Numeric (Octal) Representation**:

o   Permissions can also be set using numbers. Each permission is assigned a number:

- Read = 4
- Write = 2
- Execute = 1

o   The numbers for the owner, group, and others are combined to form a three-digit number:

- 7 (read + write + execute = 4 + 2 + 1)
- 6 (read + write = 4 + 2)
- 5 (read + execute = 4 + 1)
- 4 (read only)

o   Example: Set permissions to `rwxr-xr--` (7 for owner, 5 for group, 4 for others):

```
bash
```

```
$ sudo chmod 754 file.txt
```

Changing Ownership with `chown`

The `chown` command is used to change the ownership of a file or directory. It allows you to assign a new owner or group to the file.

1. **Changing the Owner**:
   - To change the owner of a file, use the `chown` command:

     ```bash
     $ sudo chown new_owner file.txt
     ```

2. **Changing the Group**:
   - To change the group of a file:

     ```bash
     $ sudo chown :new_group file.txt
     ```

3. **Changing Both Owner and Group**:
   - You can change both the owner and the group at the same time:

     ```bash
     ```

```
$ sudo chown new_owner:new_group
file.txt
```

4. **Viewing Ownership Information**:

   o Use the `ls -l` command to view the owner and group of a file:

   ```bash
   $ ls -l file.txt
   ```

   o Example output:

   ```diff
   -rwxr-xr-- 1 john developers 4096 Mar
   10 10:00 file.txt
   ```

   o The owner is `john`, and the group is `developers`.

Setting Special Permissions

In addition to the standard read, write, and execute permissions, there are special permissions that control specific behaviors:

1. **Setuid (Set User ID)**:

- When set on an executable file, the file runs with the permissions of the file's owner, not the user who is running the file.
- Example:

```bash
$ sudo chmod u+s /path/to/executable
```

2. **Setgid (Set Group ID)**:
   - When set on a file, the file runs with the permissions of the file's group.
   - When set on a directory, new files created in that directory inherit the group of the directory, not the user's group.
   - Example:

```bash
$ sudo chmod g+s /path/to/directory
```

3. **Sticky Bit**:
   - When set on a directory, it ensures that only the file's owner can delete or rename files within the directory, even if others have write access.
   - Example (commonly used in /tmp):

```bash
```

```
$ sudo chmod +t /path/to/directory
```

Real-World Example: Securing Web Application Files with Proper Permissions

Let's assume you're managing a web server hosting a web application. It's important to set proper permissions to ensure that the application's files are secure from unauthorized access and modification. Here's how you can secure the files:

1. **Step 1: Set Proper Permissions for Web Files**
    o   Web application files should be readable by the web server (e.g., Apache or Nginx), but only the web server should have write permissions. The owner should be able to modify the files.
    o   First, change the ownership of the application files to the web server user (e.g., `www-data` for Apache).

    bash

    ```
    $ sudo chown -R www-data:www-data /var/www/myapp
    ```

- o Then, set the following permissions:
  - The owner (`www-data`) should have full access (read, write, and execute).
  - The group (`www-data`) and others should only have read and execute permissions (so they can access the files but not modify them).
  - Use the `chmod` command to set these permissions:

```bash
$ sudo chmod -R 755 /var/www/myapp
```

2. **Step 2: Restrict Write Access to Specific Directories**
   - o For added security, restrict write permissions to specific directories, such as directories where uploaded files are stored or where logs are kept.
   - o For example, if the application has an `uploads` directory, only the web server should have write access to that directory:

```bash
$ sudo chmod 700 /var/www/myapp/uploads
```

98

3. **Step 3: Set Permissions for Sensitive Configuration Files**

   o Configuration files (e.g., `config.php`, `.env`) should be readable only by the owner and not by others. For example:

   bash

   ```
   $ sudo chmod 600 /var/www/myapp/.env
   ```

   o This ensures that only the owner (e.g., `www-data`) can read or modify the file.

4. **Step 4: Use Group Permissions for Shared Access**

   o If multiple administrators need to access the files, you can assign them to a shared group (e.g., `admins`), and set group write access:

   bash

   ```
   $ sudo chown -R :admins /var/www/myapp
   $ sudo chmod -R 770 /var/www/myapp
   ```

5. **Step 5: Regularly Review Permissions**

   o Regularly review file permissions and ownership on the web server to ensure they have not been changed or compromised.

   o Example:

```bash
$ sudo find /var/www/myapp -type f -
exec ls -l {} \;
```

Summary

In this chapter, we explored how to manage file permissions and ownership in Linux. We discussed the significance of read, write, and execute permissions, how to modify them using chmod, and how to change file ownership with chown. Additionally, we reviewed special permissions such as setuid, setgid, and sticky bits. Finally, we walked through a real-world example of securing web application files, ensuring that sensitive files are protected and that proper permissions are set for web server operations.

Mastering file permissions and ownership is essential for securing a Linux system and ensuring that only authorized users have access to critical files and directories. In the next chapter, we will explore more advanced system administration tasks such as process management and monitoring.

CHAPTER 10

PACKAGE MANAGEMENT SYSTEMS

In Linux, package management systems are essential tools that allow system administrators and users to easily install, update, and remove software. These systems simplify the process of managing software dependencies and ensure that the installed software is up-to-date and secure. In this chapter, we will cover the basics of package management using popular tools like `apt`, `yum`, and others. Additionally, we will walk through a real-world example of installing and updating a web server and database.

Package Management Overview

Linux distributions often use different package management systems depending on the package format they support. The two most common systems are:

1. **APT (Advanced Package Tool)**:
   o Used by Debian-based distributions, including **Ubuntu** and **Linux Mint**.
   o APT handles `.deb` packages and automates the installation, upgrading, and removal of software.

2. **YUM (Yellowdog Updater, Modified)**:

   o Used by Red Hat-based distributions, including **CentOS, RHEL,** and **Fedora.**

   o YUM handles .rpm packages and is responsible for managing software packages on these systems.

3. **DNF (Dandified YUM)**:

   o A newer package manager for RHEL-based distributions (used in newer versions of **Fedora** and **CentOS** 8+).

   o It's designed to be faster, more efficient, and more feature-rich than YUM.

4. **Zypper**:

   o Used by **openSUSE** distributions, handling .rpm packages.

   o Zypper can also manage software repositories and other package management tasks.

We'll focus on the two most widely used systems: **APT** and **YUM/DNF**.

APT Package Management (Debian/Ubuntu)

1. **Updating Package Lists**:

   o Before installing or updating any packages, it's essential to ensure that your package list is up-to-date. Use the following command to update the list of available packages from repositories:

```
bash


$ sudo apt update
```

2. Installing Software:

- o To install a package, use the `apt install` command followed by the package name:

```
bash


$ sudo apt install package_name
```

- o For example, to install the web server **Apache**:

```
bash


$ sudo apt install apache2
```

3. Updating Software:

- o To upgrade all installed packages to their latest versions:

```
bash


$ sudo apt upgrade
```

o This will update all packages that have updates available.

4. **Removing Software**:

   o To remove a package but keep its configuration files:

   bash

   ```
   $ sudo apt remove package_name
   ```

   o To remove a package along with its configuration files:

   bash

   ```
   $ sudo apt purge package_name
   ```

5. **Cleaning Up Unused Packages**:

   o After removing software, there may be unused packages or dependencies that are no longer required. To clean up these packages:

   bash

   ```
   $ sudo apt autoremove
   ```

6. **Searching for Packages**:

   o To search for a package in the available repositories:

```
bash
```

```
$ apt search package_name
```

YUM/DNF Package Management (RHEL/CentOS/Fedora)

1. **Updating Package Lists**:
   - o With YUM, there's no need to explicitly update the package list. However, you should periodically check for updates using the `yum` or `dnf` command.

   ```
   bash
   ```

   ```
   $ sudo yum check-update
   ```

   - o For **DNF** (newer versions of CentOS/Fedora):

   ```
   bash
   ```

   ```
   $ sudo dnf check-update
   ```

2. **Installing Software**:
   - o To install a package, use the `yum install` (for YUM) or `dnf install` (for DNF) command:

   ```
   bash
   ```

   ```
   $ sudo yum install package_name
   ```

or

```
bash
```

```
$ sudo dnf install package_name
```

- o For example, to install **Apache** on CentOS:

```
bash
```

```
$ sudo yum install httpd
```

or

```
bash
```

```
$ sudo dnf install httpd
```

3. **Updating Software**:

- o To upgrade all installed packages:

```
bash
```

```
$ sudo yum update
```

or

```
bash
```

```
$ sudo dnf upgrade
```

106

4. **Removing Software**:

o   To remove a package using YUM:

bash

```
$ sudo yum remove package_name
```

o   Using DNF:

bash

```
$ sudo dnf remove package_name
```

5. **Cleaning Up Unused Packages**:

o   To clean up YUM's cache (which can grow over time) and remove packages that are no longer needed:

bash

```
$ sudo yum autoremove
$ sudo yum clean all
```

o   For DNF:

bash

```
$ sudo dnf autoremove
$ sudo dnf clean all
```

107

6. **Searching for Packages**:

   o   To search for a package in the repositories:

   ```bash
   $ yum search package_name
   ```

   o   For DNF:

   ```bash
   $ dnf search package_name
   ```

Real-World Example: Installing and Updating a Web Server and Database

Let's walk through the steps of installing and updating a **web server** (Apache) and a **database** (MySQL) on a Linux server. This is a common task for hosting web applications.

Step 1: Install Apache Web Server

1. **On Debian-based systems (Ubuntu)**:

   ```bash
   $ sudo apt update
   $ sudo apt install apache2
   ```

2. **On RHEL-based systems (CentOS/Fedora)**:

```
bash
```

```
$ sudo yum install httpd
```

or

```
bash
```

```
$ sudo dnf install httpd
```

After installation, enable Apache to start automatically on boot:

```
bash
```

```
$ sudo systemctl enable apache2   # Debian/Ubuntu
$ sudo systemctl enable httpd           #
RHEL/CentOS/Fedora
```

Start the Apache service:

```
bash
```

```
$ sudo systemctl start apache2   # Debian/Ubuntu
$ sudo systemctl start httpd            #
RHEL/CentOS/Fedora
```

Verify Apache is running:

```
bash
```

```
$ sudo systemctl status apache2   # Debian/Ubuntu
$ sudo systemctl status httpd            #
RHEL/CentOS/Fedora
```

Open your browser and navigate to the server's IP address. You should see the Apache default page.

Step 2: Install MySQL Database Server

1. **On Debian-based systems (Ubuntu)**:

   bash

   ```
   $ sudo apt install mysql-server
   ```

2. **On RHEL-based systems (CentOS/Fedora)**:

   bash

   ```
   $ sudo yum install mysql-server
   ```

   or

   bash

   ```
   $ sudo dnf install mysql-server
   ```

Enable and start the MySQL service:

```
bash
```

```
$ sudo systemctl enable mysql
$ sudo systemctl start mysql
```

Verify that MySQL is running:

```
bash
```

```
$ sudo systemctl status mysql
```

Run the MySQL secure installation script to set a root password and secure your installation:

```
bash
```

```
$ sudo mysql_secure_installation
```

Step 3: Update Apache and MySQL

To ensure you have the latest versions of Apache and MySQL, periodically check for updates and upgrade the software.

1. **On Debian-based systems (Ubuntu)**:

   ```
   bash
   ```

   ```
   $ sudo apt update
   $ sudo apt upgrade apache2 mysql-server
   ```

2. **On RHEL-based systems (CentOS/Fedora)**:

```bash
$ sudo yum update httpd mysql-server
```

or

```bash
$ sudo dnf upgrade httpd mysql-server
```

Step 4: Remove Unused Packages

Over time, you may install and remove various software. To clean up unused packages:

1. **On Debian-based systems (Ubuntu)**:

```bash
$ sudo apt autoremove
```

2. **On RHEL-based systems (CentOS/Fedora)**:

```bash
$ sudo yum autoremove
```

or

```
bash

$ sudo dnf autoremove
```

Summary

In this chapter, we have explored the basics of package management using `apt`, `yum`, and `dnf`. We covered how to install, update, and remove software on Linux, as well as how to clean up unused packages. We also walked through a real-world example of installing and updating a web server (Apache) and a database (MySQL) on a Linux server. Mastering package management is crucial for maintaining an up-to-date and secure system. In the next chapter, we will explore process management and monitoring to ensure that your system runs smoothly.

CHAPTER 11

PROCESS MANAGEMENT AND MONITORING

In this chapter, we will explore how to view and manage processes in Linux. Understanding process management is essential for system administrators to ensure that the system is running efficiently. Linux provides several powerful tools to monitor, manage, and troubleshoot running processes. We will cover commands like `ps`, `top`, and `kill`, which are commonly used for monitoring and managing processes. Additionally, we will walk through a real-world example of monitoring a server for resource hogs and performance issues.

Viewing Running Processes

Processes are programs that are being executed on your system. Every task running in Linux is represented as a process. Below are the most common commands to view processes.

1. **`ps` (Process Status)**:
   o   The `ps` command provides information about the currently running processes. By default, `ps`

114

shows only processes running in the current terminal session.

- o Example: To view processes associated with the current session:

```
bash
```

```
$ ps
```

- ▪ Output example:

```
css
```

```
PID TTY          TIME CMD
```

1234 pts/1 00:00:00 bash 2345 pts/1 00:00:00 ps

```
pgsql
```

```
- **PID** is the Process ID, **TTY**
is the terminal type, **TIME** is the
cumulative CPU time, and **CMD** is
the command that started the process.
```

- o To view all running processes on the system:

```
bash
```

```
$ ps aux
```

- a shows processes for all users, u displays the user associated with the process, and x includes processes that are not attached to a terminal.

- Example output:

yaml

```
USER        PID %CPU %MEM    VSZ
RSS TTY       STAT START    TIME
COMMAND
root       1001  0.5  0.2 123456
7890 ?        Ss   10:00   0:03
apache2
john       2002  0.0  0.1 654321
2345 pts/1    S    10:30   0:00
bash
```

2. **top (Task Manager)**:

   o The top command provides a real-time, interactive view of system processes and resource usage, including CPU and memory utilization.

   o Example:

bash

```
$ top
```

116

- The top of the display shows CPU and memory usage, and the rest of the display lists processes. Press q to exit top.

  o Key features of top:

    - You can press M to sort processes by memory usage and P to sort by CPU usage.

    - The %CPU and %MEM columns show the percentage of CPU and memory each process is using.

3. **htop (Interactive Process Viewer)**:

  o htop is an enhanced version of top that provides a more user-friendly, interactive interface with color coding. It is not installed by default on all systems, but it can be installed via the package manager:

```
bash
```

```
$ sudo apt install htop       # Debian/Ubuntu
$ sudo yum install htop       # CentOS/RHEL
```

  o After installing, simply run:

```
bash
```

```
$ htop
```

4. pgrep (Search for Processes):

o You can use `pgrep` to search for processes by name.

o Example:

```
bash
```

```
$ pgrep apache2
```

- This returns the process IDs of all running `apache2` processes.

Managing Running Processes

1. kill (Terminate Processes):

o To terminate a process, use the `kill` command followed by the **PID** (Process ID). You can find the PID using `ps` or `top`.

o Example:

```
bash
```

```
$ kill 1234
```

- This sends a termination signal to the process with PID 1234. By default, `kill` sends the SIGTERM signal, which politely asks the process to terminate.

2. **Sending Signals**:

   o Sometimes, a process may not terminate gracefully with SIGTERM. In that case, you can use SIGKILL (signal 9), which forcefully kills the process.

   o Example:

   bash

   ```
   $ kill -9 1234
   ```

   ▪ This forcefully kills the process with PID 1234.

3. **killall (Kill Processes by Name)**:

   o If you want to kill all instances of a specific program by name (e.g., kill all apache2 processes), use the killall command:

   bash

   ```
   $ sudo killall apache2
   ```

   o This sends a termination signal to all processes with the name apache2.

4. **nice and renice (Adjusting Process Priority)**:

- o The `nice` command is used to start a process with a specified priority (nice value). A lower nice value means higher priority for the process.
- o Example:

bash

```
$ nice -n 10 command_name
```

- o You can change the priority of an already running process using `renice`:

bash

```
$ sudo renice -n 10 -p 1234
```

- o This changes the priority of the process with PID 1234.

Real-World Example: Monitoring a Server for Resource Hogs and Performance Issues

Let's walk through a real-world example of monitoring a server for resource hogs and performance issues. Suppose you are managing a server that hosts several web applications, and the server is becoming sluggish. You need to identify which processes are consuming excessive resources.

Step 1: Use `top` to Identify Resource Hogs

Run the `top` command to get an overview of the system's performance:

bash

```
$ top
```

You will see processes listed with their CPU and memory usage. Focus on the following:

- **%CPU**: Identifies how much of the CPU the process is using.
- **%MEM**: Identifies how much memory the process is consuming.
- Look for processes that have high values in these columns, especially if they are consuming resources at the expense of other processes.

Step 2: Use `htop` for a Better View

If installed, use `htop` for a more user-friendly interface:

bash

```
$ htop
```

With `htop`, you can sort processes by CPU or memory usage by pressing P for CPU or M for memory. This will help you identify which processes are consuming the most resources.

Step 3: Analyze Specific Processes

Suppose you see that the web server (`apache2`) is using excessive CPU. You can further investigate it by searching for it using `pgrep`:

```bash
$ pgrep apache2
```

This will give you a list of process IDs for the Apache server. You can then view detailed information about those processes using `ps`:

```bash
$ ps -aux | grep apache2
```

Step 4: Investigate and Kill Resource Hogs

If you find that a specific process is consuming too many resources, you may want to kill it. For example, if the process with PID 1234 is hogging resources, you can terminate it using:

bash

```
$ sudo kill 1234
```

If the process doesn't respond to SIGTERM, you can use:

bash

```
$ sudo kill -9 1234
```

Step 5: Monitor Resource Usage Over Time

You can also use tools like **sar** (System Activity Reporter) to monitor system performance over time. Install sysstat if it's not already installed:

bash

```
$ sudo apt install sysstat     # Debian/Ubuntu
$ sudo yum install sysstat     # CentOS/RHEL
```

To view CPU usage history:

bash

```
$ sar -u 1 3
```

This command shows CPU usage every second for 3 seconds.

Summary

In this chapter, we have covered the basics of process management and monitoring in Linux. We explored how to use commands like `ps`, `top`, and `htop` to view running processes, and how to use `kill` and `killall` to terminate problematic processes. We also discussed managing process priorities with `nice` and `renice`. Lastly, we provided a real-world example of monitoring a server for resource hogs and performance issues, which is a crucial task for maintaining a healthy and efficient system.

In the next chapter, we will delve into managing system services and handling system logs, two other important tasks in system administration.

CHAPTER 12

SYSTEM LOGGING AND TROUBLESHOOTING

System logs are crucial for understanding the state of your system and identifying issues that might arise during the operation of your Linux system. They contain detailed information about system events, service activities, errors, warnings, and much more. In this chapter, we will cover how to work with system logs using tools like `journalctl`, `syslog`, and others. We will also walk through a real-world example of troubleshooting a failed service using system logs.

System Logs in Linux

Logs are essential for tracking system activities, troubleshooting errors, and maintaining system health. Linux uses various logging systems to capture information about the system's operation.

1. **Systemd Journal (`journalctl`)**:
   o On modern Linux distributions that use `systemd`, logs are managed by the `journal`

service, and you can access them using the `journalctl` command.

- o The logs contain information about system events, service statuses, and kernel messages.

2. **Syslog**:

- o Older Linux systems or systems configured with `rsyslog` still use the syslog service for logging.
- o Syslog stores logs in files located in the `/var/log` directory, including files such as `/var/log/syslog`, `/var/log/messages`, and `/var/log/auth.log`.

3. **Log Files**:

- o Many services write logs to specific files in `/var/log/`. For example:
  - `/var/log/apache2/` for Apache web server logs.
  - `/var/log/mysql/` for MySQL logs.
  - `/var/log/auth.log` for authentication-related logs.

Viewing Logs with `journalctl`

`journalctl` is the primary tool for viewing logs on systems using `systemd`. It can show logs from both the kernel and user-space services, providing a comprehensive view of system events.

1. **Viewing All Logs**:
   o   To view the entire system log, simply run:

   bash

   ```
   $ journalctl
   ```

   o   This displays all the logs, starting with the oldest entries. You can scroll through them using the arrow keys or `Page Up`/`Page Down`.

2. **Viewing Logs in Reverse Order**:
   o   To see the most recent logs first, use the `-r` option:

   bash

   ```
   $ journalctl -r
   ```

   o   This will show the logs starting with the newest entries.

3. **Viewing Logs for a Specific Service**:
   o   You can filter logs by a specific service using the `-u` flag. For example, to view logs for the `apache2` service:

   bash

   ```
   $ journalctl -u apache2
   ```

127

4. **Filtering Logs by Time**:

   o You can filter logs by date using the `--since` and `--until` options:

   bash

   ```
   $ journalctl --since "2025-03-01" --until "2025-03-05"
   ```

   o This will show logs between March 1, 2025, and March 5, 2025.

5. **Real-Time Log Viewing**:

   o To view logs in real time (similar to `tail -f`), use the `-f` flag:

   bash

   ```
   $ journalctl -f
   ```

   o This will display new log entries as they are written.

6. **Limiting the Number of Log Entries**:

   o You can limit the number of log entries shown by using the `-n` option:

   bash

   ```
   $ journalctl -n 50
   ```

o   This will show the last 50 log entries.

7. **Searching Logs for Specific Keywords**:

    o   To search for specific keywords within logs, you can pipe the output of journalctl to grep:

    ```bash
    ```

    ```
    $ journalctl | grep "error"
    ```

Viewing Logs with syslog *and* rsyslog

On older systems or systems with rsyslog installed, logs are stored in plain text files in the /var/log directory.

1. **Viewing the Syslog**:

    o   To view the system log, you can use cat, less, or tail on the /var/log/syslog file:

    ```bash
    ```

    ```
    $ less /var/log/syslog
    ```

    o   The syslog contains messages about the system's general operation, including messages from various services and daemons.

2. **Viewing Authentication Logs**:

    o   Authentication   logs   are   stored   in   /var/log/auth.log and include information about user logins, sudo commands, and other authentication events:

bash

```
$ less /var/log/auth.log
```

3. **Real-Time Log Monitoring**:

   o   Use `tail` to monitor log files in real time:

   bash

   ```
   $ tail -f /var/log/syslog
   ```

   o   This will display new log entries as they are added to the file.

Real-World Example: Troubleshooting a Failed Service Using Logs

Let's say you're managing a server, and the Apache web server is not starting. Here's how you can troubleshoot the issue using logs.

Step 1: Check the Status of the Service

Start by checking the status of the Apache service with `systemctl`:

bash

```
$ sudo systemctl status apache2
```

If Apache has failed, you might see an error message indicating that the service didn't start, along with the last few log entries.

Step 2: View Apache Logs Using `journalctl`

To get more detailed information, use `journalctl` to view the Apache logs:

bash

```
$ journalctl -u apache2
```

Look for error messages or warnings that indicate the cause of the failure. Common issues might include configuration errors, missing dependencies, or permission issues.

For example, you might see something like this:

pgsql

```
Mar 10 10:00:00 myserver apache2[1234]: AH00558:
apache2: Could not reliably determine the
server's fully qualified domain name, using
127.0.0.1. Set the 'ServerName' directive
globally to suppress this message
```

131

```
Mar 10 10:00:01 myserver apache2[1234]: Syntax
error   on   line   45   of   /etc/apache2/sites-
enabled/000-default.conf:     Invalid     command
'RewriteEngine', perhaps misspelled or defined by
a module not included in the server configuration
```

This output shows two potential issues:

- Apache couldn't determine the server's fully qualified domain name (FQDN).
- There's a syntax error in the Apache configuration related to the `RewriteEngine` directive.

Step 3: Check Apache Configuration Files

The second error indicates that Apache is missing a module or the configuration is incorrect. You can check the Apache configuration files for syntax errors:

```
bash
```

```
$ sudo apache2ctl configtest
```

If there's an issue with the configuration, this command will report it. You might see something like:

```
mathematica
```

```
Syntax OK
```

132

or

```
swift
```

```
Syntax error in /etc/apache2/sites-enabled/000-
default.conf
```

Step 4: Fix the Issues

To resolve the issues:

1. For the FQDN warning, add a `ServerName` directive to the global Apache configuration:

```
bash
```

```
$ sudo nano /etc/apache2/apache2.conf
```

Add the line:

```
nginx
```

```
ServerName localhost
```

2. For the syntax error, make sure the `mod_rewrite` module is enabled:

```
bash
```

```
$ sudo a2enmod rewrite
```

Then restart Apache:

bash

```
$ sudo systemctl restart apache2
```

Step 5: Verify the Solution

Finally, check the status of the Apache service again:

bash

```
$ sudo systemctl status apache2
```

If everything is configured correctly, Apache should start without errors. You can also check the Apache logs once more to ensure that no errors are logged:

bash

```
$ journalctl -u apache2
```

Summary

In this chapter, we explored how to work with system logs in Linux using `journalctl`, `syslog`, and `rsyslog`. We covered how to view logs, filter them by time or keywords, and troubleshoot system issues using logs. We also provided a real-world example of troubleshooting a failed Apache web server service using logs, configuration tests, and corrective actions.

System logs are an invaluable resource for system administrators, helping to diagnose and resolve issues quickly. Mastering log management and troubleshooting is a key skill in maintaining a healthy and secure Linux system. In the next chapter, we will explore service management and how to configure and manage system services using `systemd`.

Part 4

Networking in Linux

CHAPTER 13

UNDERSTANDING NETWORKING BASICS

Networking is one of the core aspects of managing a Linux system, whether it's for local connections or remote access. This chapter will cover the basics of networking in Linux, including network interfaces, IP addresses, and DNS (Domain Name System). We will also walk through a real-world example of configuring a static IP for a server, which is a common task for system administrators.

Network Interfaces in Linux

A **network interface** is a software abstraction of a hardware device that allows the system to communicate over a network. Linux supports multiple network interfaces, including Ethernet (eth0, enp0s3), Wi-Fi (wlan0), and virtual interfaces (such as lo for loopback). Each interface is assigned an IP address and has specific settings related to network communication.

1. **Viewing Network Interfaces**:
    o To view all the available network interfaces on your system, use the ip command:

137

```
bash

$ ip addr
```

o   This will show a list of interfaces along with their associated IP addresses and other details.

Alternatively, you can use:

```
bash

$ ifconfig
```

o   While `ifconfig` is deprecated in many distributions, it is still widely used on older systems.

2. **Loopback Interface (lo):**

o   The loopback interface, lo, is a virtual network interface that allows the system to communicate with itself. It always uses the IP address 127.0.0.1.

o   Example:

```
bash

$ ip addr show lo
```

IP Addresses

An **IP address** (Internet Protocol address) is a unique identifier for each device on a network. There are two types of IP addresses: IPv4 and IPv6.

- **IPv4** is the most commonly used version and looks like this: `192.168.1.1`.
- **IPv6** is a newer version with a larger address space and looks like this: `fe80::f2ff:fffe:1234:abcd`.

In Linux, IP addresses can be assigned to network interfaces dynamically (using DHCP) or statically (manually).

1. **Viewing Your IP Address**:
   - You can view the IP address assigned to a specific interface by using the `ip addr` command:

     ```bash

     $ ip addr show enp0s3
     ```

   - This shows the IP address of the interface `enp0s3`. You'll find the IP address listed under the `inet` field.

2. **Assigning a Dynamic IP (DHCP)**:

139

o Most systems are configured to use **DHCP** (Dynamic Host Configuration Protocol) by default, which automatically assigns an IP address to the system.

o If you're using `systemd`-based systems, you can check the status of DHCP:

```bash
```

```
$ sudo systemctl status systemd-networkd
```

3. **Assigning a Static IP Address**:

o You may need to manually assign a static IP address to a network interface if the device requires a fixed IP address, such as a web server or database server.

o Let's walk through how to configure a static IP.

DNS (Domain Name System)

DNS is used to resolve domain names (like `example.com`) to IP addresses. It allows you to access websites and other network resources by name instead of by IP address.

1. **Viewing DNS Settings**:

o The DNS settings are typically stored in the `/etc/resolv.conf` file. You can view the DNS settings by running:

```bash
$ cat /etc/resolv.conf
```

o This file contains the IP addresses of the DNS servers used by the system.

2. **Changing DNS Settings**:

o You can manually configure DNS servers in the `/etc/resolv.conf` file. For example, to use Google's public DNS servers:

```bash
$ sudo nano /etc/resolv.conf
```

Add the following lines:

```nginx
nameserver 8.8.8.8
nameserver 8.8.4.4
```

3. **Testing DNS Resolution**:

o After configuring DNS, you can test DNS resolution with the `dig` or `nslookup` commands:

```
bash
```

```
$ dig example.com
```

o   This will query the DNS server for the IP address associated with example.com.

Real-World Example: Configuring a Static IP for a Server

Let's walk through the process of configuring a static IP address for a server. This is a common task for systems that need to have a fixed IP address to ensure they are always accessible by clients, like web servers or database servers.

Step 1: Identify Your Network Interface

First, identify the network interface you want to configure. You can list all network interfaces using the ip or ifconfig command:

```
bash
```

```
$ ip addr
```

Or:

```
bash
```

```
$ ifconfig
```

Let's assume the network interface is named enp0s3.

Step 2: Configure the Network Interface

On most systems using **netplan** (common on Ubuntu 18.04+), the network configuration files are located in the /etc/netplan/ directory. You will need to edit the relevant configuration file.

1. **Edit the Netplan Configuration File**:
   - Open the netplan configuration file (usually named 01-netcfg.yaml or something similar):

     ```bash
     $ sudo nano /etc/netplan/01-netcfg.yaml
     ```

2. **Configure Static IP**:
   - Replace the dynamic IP configuration with static IP settings. The configuration should look like this:

     ```yaml
     network:
     ```

143

```
version: 2
renderer: networkd
ethernets:
  enp0s3:
    dhcp4: no
    addresses:
      - 192.168.1.100/24
    gateway4: 192.168.1.1
    nameservers:
      addresses:
        - 8.8.8.8
        - 8.8.4.4
```

o **Explanation**:

- `dhcp4: no` disables DHCP for IPv4.

- `addresses: 192.168.1.100/24` sets the static IP address `192.168.1.100` with a subnet mask of `255.255.255.0` (`/24`).

- `gateway4: 192.168.1.1` sets the default gateway to `192.168.1.1`.

- `nameservers` specifies the DNS servers to use (Google's DNS servers in this example).

Step 3: Apply the Configuration

After making the changes, apply the new network configuration with the following command:

bash

```
$ sudo netplan apply
```

Step 4: Verify the Static IP Configuration

Verify that the static IP address has been applied by running the following command:

bash

```
$ ip addr show enp0s3
```

You should see the static IP `192.168.1.100` assigned to the `enp0s3` interface.

Step 5: Test the Network Connectivity

To ensure the server is correctly configured, try the following:

- **Ping the Gateway**:

    bash

```
$ ping 192.168.1.1
```

This ensures that the server can communicate with the gateway.

- **Test DNS Resolution**:

```
bash
```

```
$ ping google.com
```

This confirms that DNS resolution is working correctly.

Step 6: Reboot the System (Optional)

Although `netplan apply` should immediately apply the configuration, you can reboot the system to ensure that the changes are persistent across reboots:

```
bash
```

```
$ sudo reboot
```

Summary

In this chapter, we covered the basics of networking in Linux, including network interfaces, IP addresses, and DNS.

We explored tools like `ip addr`, `ifconfig`, `journalctl`, and `systemctl` to manage network settings and troubleshoot issues. We also provided a real-world example of configuring a static IP for a server, which is a common task for sysadmins.

Understanding networking basics is essential for managing Linux servers, especially in environments where static IP addresses are required for certain services. In the next chapter, we will explore managing network connections and troubleshooting network issues using advanced tools and techniques.

CHAPTER 14

MANAGING NETWORK CONNECTIONS

Network connectivity is critical for any Linux-based system, whether it's for accessing remote servers, providing services to clients, or establishing secure connections such as Virtual Private Networks (VPNs). In this chapter, we will explore how to manage network interfaces, troubleshoot connectivity issues, and configure a VPN on a Linux server. These are essential skills for anyone tasked with network administration.

Managing Network Interfaces

Network interfaces are the components of your system that allow communication with other devices on a network. Linux provides various tools to configure, monitor, and troubleshoot network interfaces.

1. **Viewing Network Interfaces**:
     o To view the network interfaces on your system, use the `ip addr` or `ifconfig` commands. These commands will show the available interfaces and their IP addresses.

```
bash

$ ip addr
```

Or:

```
bash

$ ifconfig
```

2. Example output:

3. sql

4.

5. 2:   enp0s3:
   <BROADCAST,MULTICAST,UP,LOWER_UP> mtu 1500
   qdisc fq_codel state UP qlen 1000

6.   inet   192.168.1.100/24   brd
   192.168.1.255 scope global enp0s3

7.   inet6   fe80::a00:27ff:fe6d:8b25/64
   scope link

8.   valid_lft   forever   preferred_lft
   forever

9. The IP address assigned to the `enp0s3` interface is
   192.168.1.100.

10. **Bringing Up or Down an Interface**:

    o   To bring an interface up or down, use the `ip`
        `link` command:

        ▪   Bring an interface up:

```
bash
```

```
$ sudo ip link set enp0s3 up
```

- Bring an interface down:

```
bash
```

```
$ sudo ip link set enp0s3 down
```

11. Assigning an IP Address:

- You can assign a static IP address to a network interface using the `ip addr` command:

```
bash
```

```
$ sudo ip addr add 192.168.1.101/24
dev enp0s3
```

- To remove the IP address:

```
bash
```

```
$ sudo ip addr del 192.168.1.101/24
dev enp0s3
```

12. Configuring Network Interfaces Permanently:

- In most Linux distributions, network interfaces are configured in the

150

`/etc/network/interfaces` (Debian-based) or `/etc/sysconfig/network-scripts/` (RHEL-based) files. You can edit these files to set static IP addresses, configure DNS, and more.

o Example for Debian/Ubuntu-based systems (`/etc/network/interfaces`):

```
nginx
```

```
auto enp0s3
iface enp0s3 inet static
    address 192.168.1.101
    netmask 255.255.255.0
    gateway 192.168.1.1
```

o Example for Red Hat/CentOS-based systems (`/etc/sysconfig/network-scripts/ifcfg-enp0s3`):

```
ini
```

```
DEVICE=enp0s3
BOOTPROTO=static
IPADDR=192.168.1.101
NETMASK=255.255.255.0
GATEWAY=192.168.1.1
```

13. **Checking Network Connectivity**:

   o Use the `ping` command to test network connectivity to another device on the network:

   bash

   ```
   $ ping 192.168.1.1
   ```

   o To test DNS resolution, use `ping` or `dig`:

   bash

   ```
   $ ping google.com
   $ dig google.com
   ```

Troubleshooting Connectivity Issues

Network connectivity issues can arise for various reasons, such as misconfigured interfaces, DNS problems, or network congestion. Here are a few tools and commands you can use to troubleshoot connectivity:

1. `ping`:

   o `ping` is the most basic command for testing connectivity to another device on the network. It sends ICMP Echo Request packets to a target IP address and waits for a response.

```
bash
```

```
$ ping 192.168.1.1
```

2. **traceroute**:

   o Use `traceroute` to determine the path packets take to reach a destination. This helps identify where packets are being dropped or delayed.

   ```
   bash
   ```

   ```
   $ traceroute google.com
   ```

3. **netstat**:

   o Use `netstat` to display network connections, routing tables, and interface statistics.

   ```
   bash
   ```

   ```
   $ netstat -tuln
   ```

4. **ss (Socket Stat)**:

   o `ss` is a modern alternative to `netstat` that provides similar functionality but with more efficiency and detail.

   ```
   bash
   ```

   ```
   $ ss -tuln
   ```

5. **nmcli** (NetworkManager CLI):

   o If you're using **NetworkManager** (common on desktop systems), you can use nmcli to check and manage your network connections.

   bash

   ```
   $ nmcli device status
   ```

6. **dmesg**:

   o The dmesg command shows kernel messages, which can be helpful when diagnosing hardware or network interface issues.

   bash

   ```
   $ dmesg | grep eth
   ```

Real-World Example: Setting Up a VPN on a Linux Server

A **VPN** (Virtual Private Network) provides secure communication between devices over a potentially insecure network (like the internet). In this example, we will walk through setting up **OpenVPN** on a Linux server. OpenVPN is one of the most commonly used VPN solutions on Linux.

Step 1: Install OpenVPN

First, install OpenVPN using the package manager for your Linux distribution.

1. **On Ubuntu/Debian**:

   bash

   ```
   $ sudo apt update
   $ sudo apt install openvpn
   ```

2. **On CentOS/RHEL**:

   bash

   ```
   $ sudo yum install epel-release
   $ sudo yum install openvpn
   ```

Step 2: Configure OpenVPN Server

The configuration files for OpenVPN are typically located in /etc/openvpn/. You need to configure the OpenVPN server with the appropriate settings.

1. **Create the OpenVPN Configuration File**:
   o Example configuration file (/etc/openvpn/server.conf):

155

```
pgsql

port 1194
proto udp
dev tun
ca /etc/openvpn/ca.crt
cert /etc/openvpn/server.crt
key /etc/openvpn/server.key
dh /etc/openvpn/dh2048.pem
server 10.8.0.0 255.255.255.0
ifconfig-pool-persist
/var/log/openvpn/ipp.txt
push "redirect-gateway def1"
push "dhcp-option DNS 8.8.8.8"
push "dhcp-option DNS 8.8.4.4"
keepalive 10 120
cipher AES-256-CBC
comp-lzo
user nobody
group nogroup
persist-key
persist-tun
status      /var/log/openvpn/openvpn-
status.log
log-append
/var/log/openvpn/openvpn.log
verb 3
```

o **Explanation**:

- port 1194: OpenVPN will listen on port 1194 (default).
- proto udp: The protocol is set to UDP (commonly used for VPN).
- dev tun: Specifies the use of a virtual tunnel interface.
- push "redirect-gateway def1": Redirect all client traffic through the VPN.
- push "dhcp-option DNS": Set DNS servers for the VPN clients.

2. **Enable IP Forwarding**:
   - For the server to route traffic between the VPN client and the internet, enable IP forwarding:

   bash

   ```
   $        sudo        sysctl        -w
   net.ipv4.ip_forward=1
   ```

   - To make this change permanent, edit /etc/sysctl.conf and set:

   ini

   ```
   net.ipv4.ip_forward = 1
   ```

Step 3: Start the OpenVPN Service

Once the configuration file is set up, start the OpenVPN service.

1. **On Ubuntu/Debian**:

   bash

   ```
   $ sudo systemctl start openvpn@server
   ```

2. **On CentOS/RHEL**:

   bash

   ```
   $ sudo systemctl start openvpn@server
   ```

Step 4: Configure Firewall Rules

To allow VPN traffic through the firewall, configure iptables or firewalld to permit traffic on UDP port 1194 (the default OpenVPN port).

1. **Using `iptables`**:

   bash

   ```
   $ sudo iptables -A INPUT -p udp --dport 1194 -j ACCEPT
   ```

158

```
$ sudo iptables -A FORWARD -i tun0 -j
ACCEPT
```

2. **Using `firewalld`** (for RHEL/CentOS/Fedora):

bash

```
$ sudo firewall-cmd --zone=public --add-
port=1194/udp --permanent
$ sudo firewall-cmd --zone=public --add-
interface=tun0 --permanent
$ sudo firewall-cmd --reload
```

Step 5: Verify the VPN

To verify the VPN is working, you can check the server's status and test the VPN connection from a client.

1. **Check the OpenVPN Service**:

bash

```
$ sudo systemctl status openvpn@server
```

2. **Check IP Routing**:
   o   Ensure that packets are being routed through the VPN interface:

   bash

159

```
$ ip addr show tun0
```

3. **Testing Client Connection**:

   o   On the client, try to connect to the VPN using
       the OpenVPN client:

   bash

   ```
   $ sudo openvpn --config client.ovpn
   ```

   o   If the connection is successful, verify that the
       client can access the server's internal network
       or the internet, depending on your
       configuration.

Summary

In this chapter, we discussed how to manage network
connections on Linux, including configuring network
interfaces, troubleshooting connectivity, and viewing
interface details. We also explored how to set up and manage
a VPN on a Linux server using **OpenVPN**, a commonly used
VPN solution. By mastering network management and
troubleshooting, you can ensure that your Linux systems are
properly configured and secure. In the next chapter, we will

delve deeper into advanced networking concepts such as network routing, firewalls, and VPNs.

CHAPTER 15

FIREWALL AND SECURITY CONFIGURATIONS

Firewalls are essential for securing Linux servers by controlling incoming and outgoing network traffic. Proper firewall configuration helps protect your system from unauthorized access, malicious traffic, and security threats. In this chapter, we will cover how to configure firewalls using **iptables**, **firewalld**, and **UFW** (Uncomplicated Firewall). We will also walk through a real-world example of securing an SSH server.

Configuring `iptables`

`iptables` is a powerful firewall tool used to filter network traffic on Linux. It allows administrators to define rules to allow or block traffic based on specific criteria (e.g., IP addresses, ports, protocols).

1. **Viewing Existing Rules**:
    o To view the current `iptables` rules, use the following command:

    ```bash
    bash
    ```

162

```
$ sudo iptables -L
```

2. Basic `iptables` Commands:

- o To allow incoming traffic on a specific port (e.g., port 80 for HTTP):

bash

```
$ sudo iptables -A INPUT -p tcp --
dport 80 -j ACCEPT
```

- o To block incoming traffic from a specific IP address (e.g., `192.168.1.100`):

bash

```
$ sudo iptables -A INPUT -s
192.168.1.100 -j DROP
```

3. Saving `iptables` Rules:

- o On Debian-based systems (like Ubuntu), to save the `iptables` rules:

bash

```
$ sudo iptables-save >
/etc/iptables/rules.v4
```

- o On Red Hat-based systems, use:

```bash
$ sudo service iptables save
```

4. **Resetting `iptables` Rules**:
   - o To flush (remove) all existing rules:

```bash
$ sudo iptables -F
```

5. **Example: Configuring `iptables` to Allow SSH and HTTP**:
   - o Allow incoming SSH (port 22) and HTTP (port 80) traffic:

```bash
$ sudo iptables -A INPUT -p tcp --dport 22 -j ACCEPT
$ sudo iptables -A INPUT -p tcp --dport 80 -j ACCEPT
```

   - o Deny all other incoming traffic:

```bash
```

```
$ sudo iptables -A INPUT -j DROP
```

Configuring `firewalld`

`firewalld` is a firewall management tool that uses zones to define the level of trust for network connections. It is often used in Red Hat-based distributions (such as CentOS, RHEL, and Fedora) and provides a dynamic way to manage firewall rules.

1. **Viewing Active Zones**:
    o   To check the active firewall zones:

        bash

        ```
        $ sudo firewall-cmd --get-active-zones
        ```

2. **Allowing Ports**:
    o   To allow HTTP traffic (port 80) in the `public` zone:

        bash

        ```
        $ sudo firewall-cmd --zone=public --add-port=80/tcp --permanent
        ```

    o   To allow SSH traffic (port 22):

165

bash

```
$ sudo firewall-cmd --zone=public --
add-port=22/tcp --permanent
```

3. Reloading `firewalld` to Apply Changes:

   o After adding or removing rules, reload `firewalld` to apply the changes:

bash

```
$ sudo firewall-cmd --reload
```

4. Viewing Active Rules:

   o To view the rules currently applied in the `public` zone:

bash

```
$ sudo firewall-cmd --zone=public --
list-all
```

5. Example: Securing SSH with `firewalld`:

   o Allow only SSH from a specific IP address (e.g., `192.168.1.100`):

bash

166

```
$ sudo firewall-cmd --zone=public --
add-rich-rule='rule    family="ipv4"
source address="192.168.1.100" port
protocol="tcp" port="22" accept' --
permanent
```

o   Reload firewalld:

bash

```
$ sudo firewall-cmd --reload
```

Configuring UFW (Uncomplicated Firewall)

UFW is a simpler interface for managing firewall rules on Linux. It is commonly used on Ubuntu and other Debian-based distributions. UFW provides an easy way to configure firewall rules without having to manually write iptables commands.

1. **Enabling and Checking UFW Status**:
   o   To enable UFW:

   bash

   ```
   $ sudo ufw enable
   ```

   o   To check the status of UFW:

   bash

167

```
$ sudo ufw status
```

2. Allowing Ports:

- o To allow SSH (port 22):

```
bash
```

```
$ sudo ufw allow 22
```

- o To allow HTTP (port 80):

```
bash
```

```
$ sudo ufw allow 80
```

3. Blocking Ports:

- o To block a port (e.g., blocking port 80):

```
bash
```

```
$ sudo ufw deny 80
```

4. Allowing IP Addresses:

- o To allow a specific IP address (e.g., 192.168.1.100) to access SSH:

```
bash
```

```
$ sudo ufw allow from 192.168.1.100
to any port 22
```

5. **Example: Configuring UFW for SSH and HTTP**:
   o Allow incoming SSH (port 22) and HTTP (port 80) traffic:

   bash

   ```
   $ sudo ufw allow 22
   $ sudo ufw allow 80
   ```

   o Deny all other incoming traffic:

   bash

   ```
   $ sudo ufw default deny incoming
   ```

6. **Checking UFW Status**:
   o To view the current rules:

   bash

   ```
   $ sudo ufw status verbose
   ```

Real-World Example: Securing an SSH Server

In this example, we will walk through securing an SSH server on a Linux system by configuring a firewall using iptables, `firewalld`, and `UFW` to allow only trusted users to access the server through SSH.

Step 1: Secure SSH with `iptables`

1. Allow SSH from your trusted IP (e.g., `192.168.1.100`):

bash

```
$ sudo iptables -A INPUT -s 192.168.1.100
-p tcp --dport 22 -j ACCEPT
```

2. Block all other SSH traffic:

bash

```
$ sudo iptables -A INPUT -p tcp --dport 22
-j DROP
```

3. Save the `iptables` rules to ensure they persist:

bash

```
$       sudo        iptables-save        >
/etc/iptables/rules.v4
```

Step 2: Secure SSH with `firewalld`

1. Add a rule to allow SSH from a specific IP (e.g., `192.168.1.100`):

bash

```
$ sudo firewall-cmd --zone=public --add-
rich-rule='rule family="ipv4" source
address="192.168.1.100" port
protocol="tcp" port="22" accept' --
permanent
```

2. Deny all other SSH traffic:

bash

```
$ sudo firewall-cmd --zone=public --
remove-port=22/tcp --permanent
```

3. Reload `firewalld` to apply the changes:

bash

```
$ sudo firewall-cmd --reload
```

Step 3: Secure SSH with UFW

1. Allow SSH from a trusted IP address (e.g., `192.168.1.100`):

bash

```
$ sudo ufw allow from 192.168.1.100 to any
port 22
```

2. Deny all other incoming SSH connections:

bash

```
$ sudo ufw default deny incoming
```

3. Enable the firewall if it is not already enabled:

bash

```
$ sudo ufw enable
```

4. Check the UFW status to confirm the rules:

bash

```
$ sudo ufw status verbose
```

Step 4: Test SSH Access

1. Try connecting from the trusted IP address
    (192.168.1.100):

bash

```
$ ssh user@your-server-ip
```

You should be able to connect.

2. Try connecting from a different IP address (this should be blocked):

```
bash
```

```
$ ssh user@your-server-ip
```

The connection should be denied.

Summary

In this chapter, we covered how to configure and manage firewalls using **iptables**, **firewalld**, and **UFW**. We explored basic firewall commands, including how to allow or block specific ports and IP addresses. We also provided a real-world example of securing an SSH server by restricting SSH access to trusted IP addresses using each of these firewall tools.

Configuring firewalls is a critical aspect of securing a Linux server, and understanding how to manage network connections will help prevent unauthorized access and attacks. In the next chapter, we will dive into more advanced security configurations, such as securing network services and managing security updates.

Part 5

Linux Storage Management

CHAPTER 16

REMOTE CONNECTIONS AND SSH

Secure remote management is a fundamental aspect of managing Linux servers, especially in environments where direct access to hardware is not always possible. **SSH** (Secure Shell) is a widely used protocol that allows you to securely manage remote Linux systems over an insecure network, such as the internet. In this chapter, we will explore how to use **SSH** for remote access and management, and we'll also walk through a real-world example of setting up SSH keys for secure, password-less access to your server.

Using SSH for Secure Remote Management

SSH provides a secure channel over an unsecured network by using encryption. It is a popular and essential tool for system administrators and developers to manage servers remotely. SSH ensures that the data transmitted between the client and the server is encrypted and safe from potential interception.

1. **Basic SSH Command for Remote Access**:

- To connect to a remote Linux system, you use the `ssh` command followed by the username and IP address (or hostname) of the target system:

```bash
$ ssh username@server-ip
```

- For example, if the username is `admin` and the IP address of the server is `192.168.1.10`, the command would be:

```bash
$ ssh admin@192.168.1.10
```

- Once you run the command, you'll be prompted to enter the user's password for the remote system.

2. **SSH Port**:
   - By default, SSH listens on port **22**. If you have changed the default port for security reasons, you need to specify the port using the `-p` flag:

```bash
$ ssh -p 2222 admin@192.168.1.10
```

3. **SSH Config File**:

o You can simplify frequent SSH connections by editing the SSH config file located at `~/.ssh/config` on the client machine. For example:

```bash
```

```
Host myserver
    HostName 192.168.1.10
    User admin
    Port 2222
```

o After adding this configuration, you can connect by simply typing:

```bash
```

```
$ ssh myserver
```

4. SSH Agent:

o The SSH agent stores your private SSH key so that you do not need to re-enter your passphrase every time you connect to a server. Start the agent and add your private key:

```bash
```

```
$ eval $(ssh-agent)
$ ssh-add ~/.ssh/id_rsa
```

178

5. **SSH Tunneling (Port Forwarding)**:
    o   SSH can also be used to create encrypted tunnels for other protocols. This is known as port forwarding or tunneling.
    o   For example, to forward a local port to a remote server:

    ```bash
    $ ssh -L 8080:localhost:80 user@remote-server
    ```

    o   This forwards local port 8080 to port 80 on the remote server, allowing you to securely access web services over an encrypted SSH tunnel.

Real-World Example: Setting Up SSH Keys for Secure Access

While SSH allows password-based access, using **SSH keys** is a more secure and convenient method of authentication. SSH keys eliminate the need to enter a password each time you connect and offer a higher level of security because they rely on cryptographic keys rather than a shared secret (password).

Step 1: Generate SSH Key Pair

An SSH key pair consists of two parts:

- **Private key**: Kept secret on your local machine (never shared).
- **Public key**: Can be shared and placed on the remote server.

To generate an SSH key pair, use the following command on your local machine:

1. **Generate the SSH Key Pair**:

```bash
$ ssh-keygen -t rsa -b 2048
```

- This generates a 2048-bit RSA key pair (you can choose other types like **ed25519** for more modern keys).
- When prompted for the file location, press Enter to save it in the default location (~/.ssh/id_rsa).
- You will then be asked to provide a passphrase to encrypt the private key (this is optional but recommended for added security).

2. **Key Pair Location**:
- By default, the keys will be stored in the following locations:
  - **Private key**: ~/.ssh/id_rsa

- **Public key**: `~/.ssh/id_rsa.pub`

Step 2: the Public Key to the Remote Server

Once the key pair is generated, you need to the **public key** to the remote server to allow password-less SSH access.

1. **Using `ssh--id`**:
   - The easiest way to your public key to the remote server is by using the `ssh--id` command:

   bash

   ```
   $ ssh--id username@server-ip
   ```

   - This command will prompt you for the user's password and then append your public key to the `~/.ssh/authorized_keys` file on the remote server.

2. **Manually ing the Public Key**:
   - If `ssh--id` is not available, you can manually the contents of your public key (`~/.ssh/id_rsa.pub`) to the remote server's `~/.ssh/authorized_keys` file.
   - To do this, first display the content of your public key:

   bash

181

```
$ cat ~/.ssh/id_rsa.pub
```

o   the   entire   output   and   paste   it   into   the
authorized_keys file on the remote server:

```
bash
```

```
$ ssh username@server-ip
$ mkdir -p ~/.ssh
$ echo "your-public-key-here" >>
~/.ssh/authorized_keys
$ chmod 600 ~/.ssh/authorized_keys
$ chmod 700 ~/.ssh
```

Step 3: Test SSH Key-Based Authentication

After ing your public key to the remote server, test the SSH
connection:

1. **Log in to the Server Using SSH**:
    o   If everything is set up correctly, you should
        be able to SSH into the server without being
        prompted for a password:

    ```
    bash
    ```

    ```
    $ ssh username@server-ip
    ```

o   If you provided a passphrase when generating the key pair, you will be prompted to enter it.

Step 4: Disable Password Authentication (Optional but Recommended)

To further secure the server, you can disable password-based authentication and allow only key-based authentication. This ensures that only clients with the correct private key can access the server.

1. **Edit the SSH Configuration File**:
    o   Open the SSH configuration file on the server:

```bash
$ sudo nano /etc/ssh/sshd_config
```

2. **Disable Password Authentication**:
    o   Find the following lines and modify them:

```nginx
PasswordAuthentication no
ChallengeResponseAuthentication no
```

    o   This disables password-based authentication.

3. **Restart SSH Service**:

   o After modifying the configuration file, restart the SSH service to apply the changes:

   bash

   ```
   $ sudo systemctl restart sshd
   ```

Step 5: Additional SSH Security Practices

To enhance the security of your SSH server, consider these additional measures:

1. **Change the Default SSH Port**:

   o Changing the default SSH port (22) can reduce the chances of automated attacks:

   ▪ Open the SSH configuration file (/etc/ssh/sshd_config) and change the Port line:

   yaml

   ```
   Port 2222
   ```

   ▪ Restart the SSH service:

   bash

   ```
   $ sudo systemctl restart sshd
   ```

184

- Ensure the new port is open on your firewall.

2. **Use a Firewall to Restrict SSH Access**:
   - Only allow SSH connections from trusted IP addresses by configuring your firewall (e.g., using `iptables`, `firewalld`, or `UFW`).

3. **Enable Two-Factor Authentication**:
   - For added security, you can enable two-factor authentication (2FA) for SSH access using tools like `Google Authenticator` or `Authy`.

4. **Limit SSH Access to Specific Users**:
   - Restrict SSH access to specific users by adding the following line to the SSH configuration file:

```nginx
AllowUsers username
```

Summary

In this chapter, we discussed how to use **SSH** for secure remote management of Linux systems. We covered the basic SSH command for remote access, configuring SSH key-based authentication for password-less login, and securing the SSH server by disabling password authentication. We also provided additional security measures to further protect the SSH service.

SSH is an essential tool for remotely managing Linux servers and ensuring secure communication between systems. By using SSH keys and following best practices, you can significantly enhance the security of your remote connections. In the next chapter, we will explore more advanced topics related to Linux security and auditing.

CHAPTER 17

DISK PARTITIONING AND FILESYSTEMS

Disk partitioning and filesystem management are crucial aspects of system administration. Properly configuring disk partitions, logical volume management (LVM), and filesystems ensures efficient use of storage space, system performance, and reliability. In this chapter, we will cover disk partitioning, the concept of LVM, and how to mount file systems. Additionally, we will go through a real-world example of configuring a **RAID setup** for redundancy, which provides fault tolerance by mirroring or distributing data across multiple disks.

Disk Partitioning

Disk partitioning is the process of dividing a disk into distinct sections, each treated as a separate logical unit. This allows the operating system to manage storage more effectively. Each partition can have its own filesystem, making it possible to isolate different types of data (such as system files, user data, and swap space).

1. **Viewing Existing Partitions**:
    - o To view the partitions on a disk, use the `lsblk` or `fdisk -l` commands:

    ```bash

    $ lsblk
    ```

    Or:

    ```bash

    $ sudo fdisk -l
    ```

    - o These commands display a list of all available disks and partitions, including their sizes and mount points.

2. **Creating Partitions with `fdisk`**:
    - o The `fdisk` command is used to create, delete, and manage partitions on a disk.
    - o To create a new partition on a disk (`/dev/sda`), use:

    ```bash

    $ sudo fdisk /dev/sda
    ```

    - o Inside `fdisk`, use the following commands:
        - ▪ n to create a new partition.

188

- p to print the partition table.
- w to write the changes to the disk.

3. **Creating a Swap Partition**:

   o A swap partition is used as virtual memory when the system runs out of physical RAM. To create a swap partition, follow the same procedure as creating a regular partition, then format it as swap:

   bash

   ```
   $ sudo mkswap /dev/sda3
   $ sudo swapon /dev/sda3
   ```

LVM (Logical Volume Management)

LVM provides a more flexible way to manage disk space. With LVM, you can create logical volumes (LVs) that span across multiple physical volumes (PVs). This allows for easier resizing and management of storage as compared to traditional partitioning methods.

1. **Creating Physical Volumes (PVs)**:

   o A physical volume is typically a partition or an entire disk used by LVM. To initialize a partition or disk as a physical volume:

   bash

```
$ sudo pvcreate /dev/sda1
```

2. Creating a Volume Group (VG):

- o A volume group is a pool of storage that is made up of one or more physical volumes. To create a volume group:

```
bash
```

```
$ sudo vgcreate vg_data /dev/sda1
```

- o In this example, vg_data is the name of the volume group, and /dev/sda1 is the physical volume added to the group.

3. Creating Logical Volumes (LVs):

- o Logical volumes are partitions within a volume group. They can be resized more easily than traditional partitions. To create a logical volume:

```
bash
```

```
$ sudo lvcreate -n lv_data -L 10G
vg_data
```

- o This creates a logical volume named lv_data with a size of 10 GB within the vg_data volume group.

190

4. Formatting and Mounting LVs:

o   After creating a logical volume, you can format it with a filesystem (e.g., ext4) and mount it:

bash

```
$         sudo         mkfs.ext4
/dev/vg_data/lv_data
$ sudo mount /dev/vg_data/lv_data
/mnt
```

5. Extending Logical Volumes:

o   One of the key benefits of LVM is the ability to easily extend logical volumes. For example, to extend lv_data by 5 GB:

bash

```
$     sudo     lvextend     -L     +5G
/dev/vg_data/lv_data
$             sudo             resize2fs
/dev/vg_data/lv_data
```

Mounting File Systems

Once partitions or logical volumes are created and formatted, you need to mount them to make the storage available to the system. Mounting is the process of attaching a filesystem to a directory in the system's directory tree.

191

1. **Mounting a Partition**:

   o   To mount a partition (e.g., `/dev/sda1`) to a directory (e.g., `/mnt`):

   bash

   ```
   $ sudo mount /dev/sda1 /mnt
   ```

2. **Editing `/etc/fstab` for Persistent Mounts**:

   o   To make the mount persistent across reboots, add an entry to the `/etc/fstab` file:

   bash

   ```
   $ sudo nano /etc/fstab
   ```

   o   Add a line similar to this:

   bash

   ```
   /dev/sda1    /mnt    ext4    defaults
   0    2
   ```

   o   This ensures that `/dev/sda1` is mounted to `/mnt` with the ext4 filesystem on every boot.

3. **Unmounting a File System**:

   o   To unmount a file system, use the `umount` command:

192

```
bash
```

```
$ sudo umount /mnt
```

Real-World Example: Configuring a RAID Setup for Redundancy

RAID (Redundant Array of Independent Disks) is a storage technology that combines multiple physical disks into a single logical unit for redundancy, performance, or both. In this real-world example, we will configure **RAID 1** (mirroring) for redundancy, which mirrors data across two or more disks for fault tolerance.

Step 1: Identify the Disks

First, identify the disks that will be used for the RAID setup. You can list the available disks with the `lsblk` or `fdisk -l` commands:

```
bash
```

```
$ lsblk
```

Assume the two disks are `/dev/sdb` and `/dev/sdc`.

Step 2: Install mdadm (RAID Management Tool)

To configure RAID, you need to install the mdadm utility, which is used for managing RAID arrays.

1. **On Debian/Ubuntu**:

   bash

   ```
   $ sudo apt install mdadm
   ```

2. **On CentOS/RHEL**:

   bash

   ```
   $ sudo yum install mdadm
   ```

Step 3: Create the RAID 1 Array

Use the mdadm command to create the RAID 1 array. RAID 1 mirrors data between two disks for redundancy.

1. **Create the RAID 1 Array**:

   bash

   ```
   $ sudo mdadm --create --verbose /dev/md0 --level=1 --raid-devices=2 /dev/sdb /dev/sdc
   ```

194

- o `--create`: Creates a new RAID array.

- o `--level=1`: Specifies RAID 1 (mirroring).

- o `--raid-devices=2`: Specifies the number of devices in the array.

- o `/dev/md0`: The name of the new RAID device.

- o `/dev/sdb` and `/dev/sdc`: The disks to be included in the RAID array.

2. **Monitor the RAID Creation**:

   - o Use the following command to check the status of the RAID creation:

   bash

   ```
   $ sudo cat /proc/mdstat
   ```

Step 4: Create a File System on the RAID Array

Once the RAID array is created, you need to format it with a filesystem.

1. **Format the RAID Array**:

   bash

   ```
   $ sudo mkfs.ext4 /dev/md0
   ```

Step 5: Mount the RAID Array

Next, mount the new RAID array to a directory.

1. **Mount the RAID Array**:

bash

```
$ sudo mount /dev/md0 /mnt
```

2. **Make the Mount Persistent**:

   o Edit /etc/fstab to ensure the RAID array is mounted automatically on boot:

   bash

   ```
   $ sudo nano /etc/fstab
   ```

   o Add the following line to the file:

   bash

   ```
   /dev/md0    /mnt    ext4    defaults
   0    2
   ```

Step 6: Check the RAID Status

You can check the status of the RAID array anytime using mdadm:

1. **Check RAID Array Status**:

bash

```
$ sudo mdadm --detail /dev/md0
```

2. **Monitor the RAID Array**:

- o To view the RAID array's status, you can also use:

```
bash
```

```
$ sudo cat /proc/mdstat
```

Summary

In this chapter, we covered the basics of disk partitioning, logical volume management (LVM), and mounting filesystems in Linux. We explored how to partition disks, configure LVM for flexible storage management, and mount filesystems for use. Additionally, we walked through setting up a **RAID 1** configuration for redundancy, ensuring that data is mirrored across two disks for fault tolerance. By mastering these concepts, you can effectively manage storage in a Linux environment, ensuring data integrity and system availability.

In the next chapter, we will explore advanced storage management concepts, such as managing disk quotas, file system tuning, and utilizing advanced RAID configurations for performance and scalability.

CHAPTER 18

MANAGING STORAGE VOLUMES

Managing storage volumes effectively is a crucial aspect of system administration, especially when dealing with large amounts of data or sensitive information. Logical Volume Management (LVM) is a powerful tool that provides flexibility in managing storage. In addition to LVM, encryption is an important security measure to protect sensitive data. This chapter will cover how to manage storage volumes using LVM, implement disk encryption, and walk through a real-world example of setting up encrypted partitions for sensitive data.

Logical Volume Management (LVM)

LVM allows system administrators to create a flexible and dynamic storage architecture. It provides a way to combine multiple physical disks into a single logical volume group (VG), from which logical volumes (LVs) can be created. This enables more efficient use of storage, easy resizing of volumes, and better management of disk space.

1. **Creating Physical Volumes (PVs)**:

o Physical volumes are the basic building blocks in LVM. These could be entire disks or partitions.

o To create a physical volume from a disk (e.g., `/dev/sdb`):

bash

```
$ sudo pvcreate /dev/sdb
```

2. Creating a Volume Group (VG):

o A volume group is a pool of storage that can hold multiple logical volumes.

o To create a volume group named `vg_data` from the physical volume `/dev/sdb`:

bash

```
$ sudo vgcreate vg_data /dev/sdb
```

3. Creating Logical Volumes (LVs):

o Logical volumes are created from the volume group. They function like partitions but are more flexible.

o To create a logical volume named `lv_data` with a size of 10 GB within the `vg_data` volume group:

bash

```
$ sudo lvcreate -n lv_data -L 10G
vg_data
```

4. Formatting and Mounting Logical Volumes:

- o Once a logical volume is created, it can be formatted with a filesystem and mounted.
- o To format the logical volume with the ext4 filesystem:

```
bash
```

```
$            sudo            mkfs.ext4
/dev/vg_data/lv_data
```

- o To mount the logical volume:

```
bash
```

```
$ sudo mount /dev/vg_data/lv_data
/mnt
```

5. Resizing Logical Volumes:

- o One of the key benefits of LVM is the ability to resize volumes as needed.
- o To extend the size of a logical volume by 5 GB:

```
bash
```

```
$    sudo    lvextend    -L    +5G
/dev/vg_data/lv_data
```

o   After extending the volume, resize the filesystem:

```
bash
```

```
$            sudo            resize2fs
/dev/vg_data/lv_data
```

6. **Removing Logical Volumes and Volume Groups**:

o   To remove a logical volume:

```
bash
```

```
$ sudo lvremove /dev/vg_data/lv_data
```

o   To remove a volume group (after removing all logical volumes):

```
bash
```

```
$ sudo vgremove vg_data
```

Disk Encryption

Disk encryption is crucial for protecting sensitive data from unauthorized access, especially if the disk is physically stolen or accessed without permission. **LUKS** (Linux Unified Key Setup) is the most widely used disk encryption standard on Linux. It provides encryption at the block device level, allowing entire partitions or disks to be encrypted.

1. **Encrypting a Partition with LUKS**:
   - To encrypt a partition (e.g., `/dev/sdb1`) using LUKS:

   bash

   ```
   $ sudo cryptsetup luksFormat /dev/sdb1
   ```

   - You will be prompted to confirm the action and enter a passphrase. This passphrase will be used to unlock the encrypted partition.

2. **Opening the Encrypted Partition**:
   - After encrypting the partition, you need to open it to access the data.
   - Use the following command to open the encrypted partition and map it to a logical device (e.g., `luks_data`):

   bash

   ```
   $ sudo cryptsetup luksOpen /dev/sdb1 luks_data
   ```

3. **Creating a Filesystem on the Encrypted Partition**:

- Once the partition is opened, create a filesystem (e.g., ext4):

bash

```
$           sudo           mkfs.ext4
/dev/mapper/luks_data
```

4. **Mounting the Encrypted Partition**:

- Mount the encrypted partition to a directory (e.g., `/mnt/encrypted`):

bash

```
$ sudo mount /dev/mapper/luks_data
/mnt/encrypted
```

5. **Closing the Encrypted Partition**:

- When done, close the encrypted partition:

bash

```
$    sudo    cryptsetup    luksClose
luks_data
```

6. **Adding the Encrypted Partition to /etc/crypttab for Automatic Opening**:

- To automatically open the encrypted partition during boot, add an entry to `/etc/crypttab`:

```
bash
```

```
$ sudo nano /etc/crypttab
```

o   Add a line like this:

```
nginx
```

```
luks_data /dev/sdb1 none luks
```

7. **Adding the Encrypted Partition to `/etc/fstab` for Automatic Mounting**:

o   Add the mount point for the encrypted partition to `/etc/fstab` for automatic mounting during boot:

```
bash
```

```
$ sudo nano /etc/fstab
```

o   Add a line like this:

```
pgsql
```

```
/dev/mapper/luks_data /mnt/encrypted
ext4 defaults 0 2
```

205

Real-World Example: Setting Up Encrypted Partitions for Sensitive Data

Let's walk through the steps to create an encrypted partition for storing sensitive data. This example uses **LUKS encryption** to protect the data stored on the partition, ensuring that unauthorized users cannot access it even if they have physical access to the disk.

Step 1: Identify the Partition

Identify the disk or partition you want to encrypt (e.g., /dev/sdb1). Use lsblk to list the available disks and partitions:

bash

```
$ lsblk
```

Step 2: Encrypt the Partition Using LUKS

1. To encrypt /dev/sdb1:

    bash

    ```
    $ sudo cryptsetup luksFormat /dev/sdb1
    ```

2. Confirm the action and set a secure passphrase.

206

Step 3: Open the Encrypted Partition

1. Open the encrypted partition to make it accessible:

bash

```
$ sudo cryptsetup luksOpen /dev/sdb1
luks_sensitive_data
```

Step 4: Create a Filesystem on the Encrypted Partition

1. Create a filesystem (ext4) on the opened encrypted partition:

bash

```
$ sudo mkfs.ext4
/dev/mapper/luks_sensitive_data
```

Step 5: Mount the Encrypted Partition

1. Create a mount point and mount the encrypted partition:

bash

```
$ sudo mkdir /mnt/sensitive_data
$ sudo mount
/dev/mapper/luks_sensitive_data
/mnt/sensitive_data
```

Step 6: Configure Automatic Unlocking and Mounting

1. Add the encrypted partition to `/etc/crypttab` for automatic unlocking at boot:

bash

```
$ sudo nano /etc/crypttab
```

Add the following line:

nginx

```
luks_sensitive_data /dev/sdb1 none luks
```

2. Add the mount point to `/etc/fstab` for automatic mounting:

bash

```
$ sudo nano /etc/fstab
```

Add the following line:

bash

```
/dev/mapper/luks_sensitive_data
/mnt/sensitive_data ext4 defaults 0 2
```

Step 7: Test the Configuration

1. Reboot the system to test that the encrypted partition is automatically unlocked and mounted:

bash

```
$ sudo reboot
```

2. After the system reboots, verify that the encrypted partition is mounted:

bash

```
$ df -h /mnt/sensitive_data
```

Summary

In this chapter, we discussed **Logical Volume Management (LVM)**, which allows for flexible disk management, and **disk encryption** using **LUKS** to secure sensitive data. We covered how to create physical volumes, volume groups, and logical volumes using LVM, and how to set up encrypted partitions to protect sensitive information.

LVM provides flexibility and scalability for managing storage, while disk encryption ensures that even if the physical device is compromised, the data remains secure. By understanding these concepts, you can effectively manage and secure data on Linux systems.

In the next chapter, we will explore advanced storage management techniques, such as managing disk quotas, file system performance tuning, and handling storage failures.

CHAPTER 19

DISK USAGE AND CLEANUP

As a Linux system administrator, managing disk space efficiently is essential to ensure that your system runs smoothly. Over time, systems can accumulate unnecessary files that take up valuable disk space, leading to performance issues or even preventing the system from functioning properly. In this chapter, we will explore tools and techniques to identify large files, clean up unnecessary files, and free up disk space. We will also walk through a real-world example of cleaning up a server after a large deployment.

Finding Large Files

Finding large files that are taking up disk space is one of the first steps in cleaning up a system. Linux provides several utilities to help you identify these files.

1. **Using the du (Disk Usage) Command**:
    o   The du command is used to estimate file space usage. By default, it shows the disk usage of the current directory and its subdirectories.

```
bash
```

```
$ du -h
```

o   The -h flag makes the output human-readable, showing sizes in KB, MB, GB, etc.

2. Finding the Largest Directories:

o   To find the largest directories within a specific path, use the following command:

```
bash
```

```
$      du      -h      --max-depth=1
/path/to/directory
```

o   The --max-depth=1 option limits the output to only the top-level directories, making it easier to find large folders. You can increase the depth if you want to explore subdirectories.

3. Finding the Largest Files:

o   The find command can be combined with du or ls to locate large files. For example, to find files larger than 100 MB:

```
bash
```

```
$ find /path/to/directory -type f -
size +100M
```

o   This will list all files over 100 MB in the specified directory.

4. **Using ncdu (NCurses Disk Usage)**:

o   ncdu is an interactive, text-based utility that makes it easy to navigate through directories and find large files.

o   To install ncdu (on Debian/Ubuntu):

bash

```
$ sudo apt install ncdu
```

o   Once installed, run it on a directory (e.g., /var):

bash

```
$ sudo ncdu /var
```

o   ncdu will show the disk usage in an easy-to-read interface, and you can navigate through directories interactively.

5. **Finding Files Based on Age**:

o   Sometimes, you want to find old files that are no longer needed. To find files older than a certain number of days (e.g., 30 days), you can use the find command:

bash

```
$ find /path/to/directory -type f -
mtime +30
```

o This command finds all files in /path/to/directory that haven't been modified in the last 30 days.

Cleaning Up Unnecessary Files

Once you've identified large or unnecessary files, the next step is to clean them up. There are several ways to do this in Linux.

1. **Removing Unnecessary Files**:

    o Once you identify unnecessary files, you can remove them using the rm command. For example, to remove a specific file:

    bash

    ```
    $ sudo rm /path/to/file
    ```

    o To remove a directory and all its contents (use with caution):

    bash

    ```
    $ sudo rm -r /path/to/directory
    ```

2. **Clearing Package Cache**:

   o   Package managers, such as `apt` or `yum`, often store downloaded package files in cache directories, which can accumulate over time.

   o   For **APT** (Debian/Ubuntu-based systems):

   bash

   ```
   $ sudo apt-get clean
   ```

   - This removes all cached package files from `/var/cache/apt/archives`.

   o   For **YUM** (Red Hat/CentOS-based systems):

   bash

   ```
   $ sudo yum clean all
   ```

   - This removes cached data stored in `/var/cache/yum`.

3. **Removing Old Log Files**:

   o   Log files can take up significant space, especially on servers with extensive logging. You can remove old log files that are no longer necessary.

   o   To clear the contents of a log file (but keep the file itself):

   bash

215

```
$ sudo truncate -s 0 /var/log/syslog
```

o   To remove old logs:

bash

```
$ sudo rm /var/log/*.gz
```

4. **Using tmpwatch to Clean Temporary Files**:

o   Temporary files are stored in /tmp and /var/tmp. These files often accumulate over time and can be safely removed.

o   Install and use tmpwatch (on CentOS/RHEL):

bash

```
$ sudo yum install tmpwatch
$ sudo tmpwatch --mtime --all 72 /tmp
```

o   This command removes files in /tmp that haven't been accessed in the last 72 hours.

5. **Removing Orphaned Packages**:

o   Orphaned packages are packages that were installed as dependencies but are no longer required. You can remove them to free up space.

o   For **APT**:

```
bash
```

```
$ sudo apt-get autoremove
```

- o For **YUM**:

```
bash
```

```
$ sudo package-cleanup --quiet --
leaves --exclude-bin
```

6. **Removing Old Kernel Versions**:

- o Older kernel versions can take up significant disk space. It's safe to remove older kernel versions if you're sure that the system is running the latest kernel.

- o To list installed kernels:

```
bash
```

```
$ dpkg --list | grep linux-image
```

- o To remove an old kernel:

```
bash
```

```
$ sudo apt-get remove --purge linux-
image-X.X.X-XX-generic
```

Real-World Example: Cleaning Up a Full Server After a Large Deployment

Imagine a scenario where you've just completed a large deployment on a Linux server, and now the disk is full. Here's how you can clean up the server to free up space.

Step 1: Identify Large Files and Directories

1. Run `ncdu` to get an interactive view of disk usage:

```bash
$ sudo ncdu /
```

2. Identify large directories that are taking up space, such as log directories or temporary files.

Step 2: Clean Up Package Cache

1. Clear the APT cache to remove unnecessary downloaded package files:

```bash
$ sudo apt-get clean
```

Step 3: Remove Old Log Files

1. Clear old log files that are no longer needed:

```
bash
```

```
$ sudo rm /var/log/*.gz
$ sudo truncate -s 0 /var/log/syslog
```

Step 4: Remove Old Kernel Versions

1. List the installed kernels and remove old versions:

```
bash
```

```
$ dpkg --list | grep linux-image
$ sudo apt-get remove --purge linux-image-
4.15.0-20-generic
```

Step 5: Remove Orphaned Packages

1. Remove orphaned packages that are no longer needed:

```
bash
```

```
$ sudo apt-get autoremove
```

Step 6: Clean Temporary Files

1. Use tmpwatch (or equivalent) to clean up old temporary files:

```
bash
```

```
$ sudo tmpwatch --mtime --all 72 /tmp
```

219

Step 7: Verify Disk Space

1. After cleaning up, verify the available disk space:

```bash

$ df -h
```

This should show that your disk space has been freed up significantly.

Summary

In this chapter, we explored how to identify large files, clean up unnecessary files, and free up disk space on a Linux system. We discussed tools like du, find, ncdu, and commands like apt-get clean, tmpwatch, and autoremove to remove unwanted files, old logs, package caches, and orphaned packages. We also provided a real-world example of cleaning up a server after a large deployment, focusing on key steps such as removing old log files, clearing package caches, and freeing space occupied by old kernel versions.

Efficient disk usage management is crucial for maintaining system performance and avoiding disk-related issues. By using these tools and techniques, you can ensure that your Linux systems have enough free space to run smoothly and securely.

In the next chapter, we will dive deeper into advanced disk usage management, including disk quotas, filesystem tuning, and optimizing storage for better performance.

CHAPTER 20

BACKUP AND RESTORE STRATEGIES

Backup and restore strategies are critical for ensuring the safety of data on your Linux systems. Whether you're maintaining personal data, databases, or entire server configurations, having a solid backup plan is essential to avoid data loss due to hardware failures, human errors, or disasters. In this chapter, we will cover essential backup tools and strategies for Linux, such as **rsync** and **tar**, and show you how to automate regular backups. We will also walk through a real-world example of automating weekly backups of a server's data.

Backup Tools for Linux

1. **rsync**:
   o **rsync** is one of the most powerful and versatile tools for making backups. It efficiently copies and synchronizes files and directories between two locations, whether on the same machine or over a network. rsync only copies the differences between the

source and destination, making it highly efficient.

o **Basic rsync Command**:

bash

```
$ rsync -av /source/directory
/destination/directory
```

- -a (archive) preserves the structure and attributes of files.
- -v (verbose) provides detailed output of the file transfer process.

o **Remote Backup with rsync**:

- To backup files to a remote server, you can use rsync over SSH:

bash

```
$ rsync -avz /local/directory
username@remote-
server:/remote/directory
```

- -z compresses the data during transfer, which is useful for reducing bandwidth usage.

o **Excluding Files or Directories**:

223

- You can exclude specific files or directories from being backed up:

```bash
$ rsync -av --exclude '*.log'
/source/directory
/destination/directory
```

2. **tar**:

   o The **tar** command (short for tape archive) is commonly used to create compressed backup archives. You can use it to back up entire directories or individual files into a single archive file.

   o **Creating a tar Backup**:

```bash
$ tar -czvf backup.tar.gz
/path/to/directory
```

     - -c creates an archive.
     - -z compresses the archive using gzip.
     - -v provides verbose output.
     - -f specifies the filename for the archive.

   o **Restoring a tar Backup**:
     - To extract files from a tar archive:

224

```
bash
```

```
$ tar -xzvf backup.tar.gz
```

o **Backing Up and Compressing Multiple Directories**:

```
bash
```

```
$ tar -czvf backup.tar.gz
/path/to/dir1 /path/to/dir2
```

3. **cp ()**:

  o The cp command can also be used to create backups by ing files or directories to another location.

  o **Basic Command**:

```
bash
```

```
$ cp -r /source/directory
/destination/directory
```

  ▪ The -r option is used to directories recursively.

4. **dd**:

  o The **dd** command is used to create low-level, byte-for-byte backups of disks or partitions. It's

225

commonly used for creating disk images or cloning a drive.

o **Creating a Disk Image**:

```bash
$      sudo      dd      if=/dev/sda
of=/path/to/backup.img bs=64K
```

- `if` specifies the input file (e.g., a disk or partition).
- `of` specifies the output file (e.g., backup image).
- `bs` defines the block size for the transfer.

5. **Backup Software (GUI Tools)**:
   o For users who prefer graphical user interfaces (GUIs), tools like **Deja Dup** (for GNOME), **Timeshift**, and **KBackup** provide easy-to-use backup solutions.

Backup Strategies for Linux

1. **Full Backups**:
   o A full backup involves ing all files from the source to the backup location. While this provides the most comprehensive backup, it requires significant storage space and can take a long time to complete.

- o Full backups should be done periodically, especially for important data.

2. **Incremental Backups**:

   - o An incremental backup only backs up files that have changed since the last backup. This is much faster than full backups and requires less storage.
   - o **rsync** is perfect for incremental backups because it only copies changes made to the files since the last backup.

3. **Differential Backups**:

   - o A differential backup is similar to an incremental backup, but instead of backing up files changed since the last backup, it backs up files changed since the last full backup. This takes more space than an incremental backup but is faster than a full backup.

4. **Backup Rotation**:

   - o To manage storage efficiently, you can use a backup rotation strategy, such as the **Grandfather-Father-Son** model. In this model:
     - **Son** backups are daily backups.
     - **Father** backups are weekly backups.
     - **Grandfather** backups are monthly backups.

o This method ensures you have backups for a reasonable period without consuming excessive storage space.

Real-World Example: Automating Weekly Backups of a Server's Data

Let's walk through a scenario where we automate weekly backups of a server's data using **rsync** and **cron**, a Linux utility that schedules tasks to run at specific times.

Step 1: Setting Up the Backup Script

1. Create a backup script that will use `rsync` to back up data from the server's `/home` directory to an external backup directory or remote server.

bash

```
$ nano /usr/local/bin/backup.sh
```

Add the following content to the script:

bash

```
#!/bin/bash
# Backup source and destination directories
SOURCE="/home"
```

```
DEST="/backup"

# Perform the backup with rsync
rsync -avz --exclude 'cache/' --exclude
'*.log' $SOURCE $DEST
```

- o This script uses `rsync` to back up the `/home` directory to `/backup`. It excludes directories like `cache/` and files with the `.log` extension.

2. Make the script executable:

```
bash
```

```
$ sudo chmod +x /usr/local/bin/backup.sh
```

Step 2: Scheduling the Backup with `cron`

1. Edit the crontab to schedule the backup script to run weekly:

```
bash
```

```
$ sudo crontab -e
```

2. Add a line to the crontab to run the script every Sunday at 2 AM:

```
swift
```

```
0 2 * * 0 /usr/local/bin/backup.sh
```

o   This cron job will run the backup script at 2:00 AM every Sunday (0 represents Sunday).

3. Save and close the crontab file. The cron daemon will automatically pick up the new schedule.

Step 3: Verifying the Backup Process

1. To verify the backup is working as expected, you can manually trigger the cron job to run immediately:

bash

```
$ sudo /usr/local/bin/backup.sh
```

2. Check the backup directory (/backup) to ensure that the files are being backed up correctly.

Step 4: Monitoring and Logging the Backups

1. To log the output of the backup process for future reference, modify the backup script to redirect the output to a log file:

bash

```
#!/bin/bash
# Backup source and destination directories
SOURCE="/home"
```

```
DEST="/backup"
LOGFILE="/var/log/backup.log"

# Perform the backup with rsync and log the
output
rsync -avz --exclude 'cache/' --exclude
'*.log' $SOURCE $DEST >> $LOGFILE 2>&1
```

2. Check the log file to ensure that the backup process runs correctly:

```bash
$ tail -f /var/log/backup.log
```

Summary

In this chapter, we discussed essential backup tools and strategies for Linux, focusing on **rsync**, **tar**, and other utilities such as **cp** and **dd**. We explored various backup strategies, including full, incremental, and differential backups, and we highlighted the importance of backup rotation for long-term data management.

We also walked through a real-world example of automating weekly backups of a server's data using **rsync** and **cron**.

231

This solution ensures that critical server data is regularly backed up, with logs available for troubleshooting.

By implementing effective backup strategies and automating the process, system administrators can ensure that their data is always protected, and recovery from failure is quick and reliable. In the next chapter, we will delve into more advanced backup techniques, including cloud backups, offsite storage, and disaster recovery planning.

Part 6

Advanced System Administration

CHAPTER 21

PERFORMANCE TUNING AND OPTIMIZATION

As a system administrator, one of your key responsibilities is ensuring that your system runs efficiently and can handle the workloads it faces. Performance tuning and optimization help improve system speed, responsiveness, and resource utilization, ensuring that applications, databases, and services perform optimally. This chapter will cover techniques for optimizing the CPU, memory, disk, and network. We will also look at a real-world example of optimizing a database server for high load.

Optimizing CPU Performance

The CPU is one of the most critical components of a system, and its performance can significantly affect the overall system efficiency. Optimizing CPU performance involves identifying resource hogs and fine-tuning the system to ensure it runs at peak efficiency.

1. **Monitoring CPU Usage**:
    o   Use the `top` or `htop` command to monitor CPU usage in real-time.

```
bash
```

```
$ top
```

o The %CPU column shows the percentage of CPU usage by each process. Look for processes that are using a high percentage of CPU resources.

2. **Managing CPU Affinity**:

o CPU affinity allows you to bind a process to a specific CPU core. This can improve performance in multi-core systems by reducing CPU cache misses.

```
bash
```

```
$ taskset -c 0,1 myprocess
```

o This command binds myprocess to CPU cores 0 and 1.

3. **Reducing CPU Load**:

o Use tools like **nice** and **renice** to adjust the priority of processes:

- **nice** sets the priority of a new process:

```
bash
```

```
$ nice -n 10 command
```

- **renice** adjusts the priority of a running process:

bash

```
$ sudo renice -n 10 -p 1234
```

4. Disabling Unnecessary Services:

- Identify and disable services that are consuming CPU resources unnecessarily.
- List running services:

bash

```
$ systemctl list-units --type=service
```

- Disable unneeded services:

bash

```
$ sudo systemctl disable some-service
```

5. CPU Frequency Scaling:

- Enable CPU frequency scaling to adjust the CPU's performance based on system demand. Tools like **cpupower** can help manage this:

```
bash
```

```
$ sudo cpupower frequency-set --
governor performance
```

Optimizing Memory Usage

Efficient memory usage is key to maintaining a responsive and stable system. Optimizing memory involves both managing how memory is used and ensuring that the system doesn't run out of memory.

1. **Monitoring Memory Usage**:
   o Use `free` or `vmstat` to monitor system memory usage:

   ```
   bash
   ```

   ```
   $ free -h
   $ vmstat
   ```

2. **Reducing Memory Usage**:
   o **Clear Page Cache**: Linux uses disk space as virtual memory (swap). Over time, the page cache can consume significant memory. To clear the page cache:

   ```
   bash
   ```

```
$ sudo sync
$       sudo      echo      3      >
/proc/sys/vm/drop_caches
```

3. **Identifying Memory Leaks**:
   o Use **top** or **htop** to identify processes with unusually high memory usage. Look for processes that consistently consume more memory over time.
   o Tools like **smem** provide a detailed breakdown of memory usage by process:

   bash

   ```
   $ sudo apt install smem
   $ smem -rs rss
   ```

4. **Optimizing Swapping and Virtual Memory**:
   o Adjust the **swappiness** value to control how much the kernel favors using swap space:

   bash

   ```
   $ sudo sysctl vm.swappiness=10
   ```

   o To make the change permanent, add it to /etc/sysctl.conf.

Optimizing Disk Performance

Disk performance can become a bottleneck, especially when dealing with large databases, file servers, or media-heavy applications. Optimizing disk usage and speed can lead to significant performance improvements.

1. **Monitoring Disk Usage**:
   - Use `iostat` or `iotop` to monitor disk I/O:

   bash

   ```
   $ iostat -x 1
   $ sudo iotop
   ```

2. **Reducing Disk I/O with `noatime`**:
   - The **atime** attribute updates each time a file is accessed. Disabling this can reduce disk write operations, especially on systems that read a lot of files.
   - Add the `noatime` option to `/etc/fstab` for the relevant file systems:

   bash

   ```
   /dev/sda1  /  ext4  defaults,noatime
   0  1
   ```

3. **Optimizing Disk Access Patterns**:

  o For workloads with heavy read/write operations, consider using a **RAID** setup to distribute the load across multiple disks. RAID 0 (striping) improves read and write speeds, while RAID 1 (mirroring) provides redundancy.

4. **Using Solid-State Drives (SSDs)**:

  o SSDs significantly improve read/write speeds compared to traditional hard drives (HDDs). If the system is using HDDs, consider upgrading to SSDs for better performance.

5. **Using Filesystem Tuning Parameters**:

  o Tune filesystem parameters for better performance. For example, the **ext4** filesystem has the `nojournal` option to disable journaling (useful for certain workloads like databases):

```bash
/dev/sda1          /          ext4
defaults,nojournal  0  1
```

Optimizing Network Performance

Network performance is vital for systems that rely on external communication, such as web servers, database servers, or cloud-based applications. Optimizing the network ensures faster communication and reduces latency.

1. **Monitoring Network Usage**:
   - Use **netstat** or **ss** to monitor network connections and the status of network interfaces:

   bash

   ```
   $ netstat -tuln
   $ ss -tuln
   ```

2. **Reducing Latency with TCP Optimizations**:
   - **Increase the TCP buffer size** to accommodate higher bandwidth:

   bash

   ```
   $ sudo sysctl -w
   net.core.rmem_max=16777216
   $ sudo sysctl -w
   net.core.wmem_max=16777216
   ```

   - These commands increase the maximum receive and send buffer size for TCP connections.

3. **Adjusting TCP Congestion Control Algorithm**:
   - Different congestion control algorithms optimize different aspects of network communication. For example, **CUBIC** is suitable for high-bandwidth, low-latency environments, while **BBR** is better for congestion control.

241

```
bash
```

```
$        sudo        sysctl        -w
net.ipv4.tcp_congestion_control=bbr
```

4. **Offloading Tasks to the Network Interface Card (NIC)**:
   o Enable offload features on the NIC to reduce the CPU load and increase network throughput. For example:

```
bash
```

```
$ sudo ethtool -K eth0 tso off
```

Real-World Example: Optimizing a Database Server for High Load

Imagine you're managing a database server running MySQL or PostgreSQL that has to handle a high load of database queries. Here's how you can optimize the system:

Step 1: CPU and Memory Optimization

1. **Adjust MySQL or PostgreSQL Configuration**:
   o Increase the buffer pool size for MySQL:

```
bash
```

```
$ sudo nano /etc/mysql/my.cnf
```

- Increase the innodb_buffer_pool_size to a higher percentage of system memory (e.g., 70%).

2. **Optimize Memory Usage for Query Caching**:

   o Enable or increase query cache size in MySQL:

   bash

   ```
   $ sudo nano /etc/mysql/my.cnf
   ```

   - Set query_cache_size to a suitable value (e.g., 64M).

3. **Use SSD Storage for Database Files**:

   o If the server uses HDDs, consider moving the database files to SSDs for faster read/write speeds.

Step 2: Disk I/O Optimization

1. **Use RAID Configuration**:

   o For better disk performance and redundancy, set up RAID 10, which offers a good balance between speed and fault tolerance.

2. **Optimize Filesystem**:

   o Use **XFS** or **ext4** filesystems with optimized parameters for database workloads:

- Mount the database directory with `noatime` to prevent unnecessary disk writes.

1. **TCP Optimization**:
   o Enable **TCP BBR** to optimize throughput:

   bash

   ```
   $    sudo    sysctl    -w
   net.ipv4.tcp_congestion_control=bbr
   ```

2. **Increase Network Buffer Size**:
   o Increase network buffer sizes to accommodate high traffic:

   bash

   ```
   $    sudo    sysctl    -w
   net.core.rmem_max=16777216
   $    sudo    sysctl    -w
   net.core.wmem_max=16777216
   ```

3. **Limit Unnecessary Services**:
   o Disable unnecessary services to free up network bandwidth and CPU resources, ensuring that all

244

available resources are used for the database service.

Summary

In this chapter, we explored techniques for optimizing CPU, memory, disk, and network performance in Linux. We discussed tools and strategies to monitor and improve system performance, including adjusting system settings, configuring storage systems, and optimizing network traffic. We also provided a real-world example of optimizing a database server to handle high loads by adjusting system configurations, utilizing SSDs, and tuning network settings.

Performance tuning is a continuous process that requires monitoring, adjustments, and fine-tuning to ensure that your systems perform optimally under various loads. In the next chapter, we will delve deeper into advanced system administration topics, including managing large-scale deployments and automating administrative tasks.

CHAPTER 22

VIRTUALIZATION AND CONTAINERS

Virtualization and containerization have become essential technologies for modern systems administration, enabling efficient resource utilization, isolation, and scalability. Virtualization allows multiple virtual machines (VMs) to run on a single physical machine, while containers provide a lightweight alternative that focuses on packaging applications and their dependencies into isolated environments. In this chapter, we will explore tools like **Docker**, **LXD**, and **KVM** for virtualization, and provide a real-world example of setting up a containerized application using **Docker**.

Using Docker

Docker is one of the most popular tools for containerization. It allows developers and system administrators to package applications and their dependencies into portable, isolated containers. Containers are lightweight and start quickly, making them ideal for microservices, CI/CD pipelines, and cloud-native applications.

1. **Installing Docker**:

   o   To install Docker on Ubuntu, use the following commands:

   ```bash
   $ sudo apt update
   $ sudo apt install docker.io
   ```

   o   For CentOS/RHEL:

   ```bash
   $ sudo yum install docker
   ```

2. **Starting Docker**:

   o   Enable and start the Docker service:

   ```bash
   $ sudo systemctl enable docker
   $ sudo systemctl start docker
   ```

3. **Docker Images and Containers**:

   o   **Docker Image**: A Docker image is a read-only template that contains the application and its dependencies.

o **Docker Container**: A container is an instance of a Docker image that runs in isolation.

o To pull a Docker image from Docker Hub:

bash

```
$ sudo docker pull ubuntu
```

o To run a container from the pulled image:

bash

```
$ sudo docker run -it ubuntu
```

o This command runs an interactive Ubuntu container. The `-it` flags make the container interactive and allocate a terminal to it.

4. **Managing Docker Containers**:

o List running containers:

bash

```
$ sudo docker ps
```

o List all containers (including stopped ones):

bash

```
$ sudo docker ps -a
```

o   To stop a running container:

bash

```
$ sudo docker stop <container_id>
```

o   To remove a container:

bash

```
$ sudo docker rm <container_id>
```

5. **Building Docker Images**:

o   Docker images can be built from a `Dockerfile`, which contains instructions for building the image.

o   Example `Dockerfile`:

sql

```
FROM ubuntu:latest
RUN apt-get update && apt-get install
-y python3 python3-pip
CMD ["python3"]
```

o   To build the image:

249

```
bash
```

```
$ sudo docker build -t my-python-app
.
```

6. Docker Compose:

- Docker Compose is a tool for defining and running multi-container Docker applications.
- Define your services in a docker-compose.yml file. Example docker-compose.yml:

```yaml
version: '3'
services:
  web:
    image: nginx
    ports:
      - "80:80"
```

- To start the application:

```
bash
```

```
$ sudo docker-compose up
```

Using LXD for System Containers

LXD is a system container manager that provides an easy way to run Linux distributions in containers. Unlike Docker, which focuses on packaging applications, LXD allows you to create containers that act like virtual machines but with better performance and less overhead.

1. **Installing LXD**:
   - On Ubuntu:

   bash

   ```
   $ sudo apt install lxd
   ```

2. **Initializing LXD**:
   - Initialize LXD to set up storage pools and networking:

   bash

   ```
   $ sudo lxd init
   ```

3. **Creating Containers with LXD**:
   - To create a container running Ubuntu:

   bash

251

```
$ sudo lxc launch ubuntu:20.04 my-
container
```

o List containers:

```
bash
```

```
$ sudo lxc list
```

4. **Managing Containers with LXD**:

o To enter a running container:

```
bash
```

```
$ sudo lxc exec my-container -- bash
```

o To stop and delete a container:

```
bash
```

```
$ sudo lxc stop my-container
$ sudo lxc delete my-container
```

Using Virtualization Tools: KVM and VirtualBox

1. **KVM (Kernel-based Virtual Machine)**:

o KVM is a Linux kernel module that enables hardware virtualization. It is one of the most powerful virtualization options available on Linux.

252

- **Installing KVM**:
  - Install KVM and associated tools:

    bash

    ```
    $ sudo apt install qemu-kvm
    libvirt-daemon-system libvirt-
    clients bridge-utils
    ```

  - Add your user to the `libvirt` group to manage virtual machines:

    bash

    ```
    $ sudo usermod -aG libvirt
    $USER
    ```

- **Managing Virtual Machines with `virt-manager`**:
  - Install `virt-manager` to use a GUI to manage virtual machines:

    bash

    ```
    $ sudo apt install virt-
    manager
    ```

- **Creating Virtual Machines**:

- You can create and manage virtual machines using the `virt-manager` GUI or the command line with `virsh`.

2. **VirtualBox**:

   o **VirtualBox** is a cross-platform virtualization tool that provides a graphical interface to create and manage virtual machines.

   o **Installing VirtualBox**:

   ```bash
   $ sudo apt install virtualbox
   ```

   o **Managing Virtual Machines**:

   - Use the **VirtualBox GUI** to create and manage virtual machines, or use the `VBoxManage` command-line tool:

   ```bash
   $ VBoxManage createvm --name "MyVM" --register
   ```

   o VirtualBox is particularly useful when you need a GUI-based solution for creating and managing virtual machines.

Real-World Example: Setting Up a Containerized Application Using
Docker

Let's walk through a real-world example of setting up a containerized application using Docker. For this example, we will deploy a simple **Nginx web server** inside a Docker container.

Step 1: Install Docker

1. Install Docker on your system:

   bash

   ```
   $ sudo apt update
   $ sudo apt install docker.io
   ```

2. Enable Docker to start at boot and start the service:

   bash

   ```
   $ sudo systemctl enable docker
   $ sudo systemctl start docker
   ```

Step 2: Pull the Nginx Image from Docker Hub

1. Pull the official **Nginx** image from Docker Hub:

   bash

```
$ sudo docker pull nginx
```

Step 3: Run the Nginx Container

1. Start the Nginx container:

```bash
$ sudo docker run -d -p 80:80 --name my-nginx nginx
```

- o   -d runs the container in detached mode (in the background).
- o   -p 80:80 maps port 80 of the host to port 80 of the container.
- o   --name my-nginx assigns the name my-nginx to the container.

2. To verify the container is running:

```bash
$ sudo docker ps
```

3. Open a web browser and navigate to http://localhost. You should see the default Nginx welcome page.

Step 4: Modify the Nginx Configuration

1. To modify the Nginx configuration, first stop the container:

bash

```
$ sudo docker stop my-nginx
```

2. Create a custom Nginx configuration file:

bash

```
$ sudo nano nginx.conf
```

- o Add the following content to `nginx.conf`:

nginx

```
server {
    listen 80;
    server_name localhost;
    location / {
        root /usr/share/nginx/html;
        index index.html;
    }
}
```

3. Start a new container using the custom configuration:

bash

```
$ sudo docker run -d -p 80:80 --name my-
nginx                                    -v
/path/to/nginx.conf:/etc/nginx/nginx.conf
nginx
```

- o The -v flag mounts the custom nginx.conf file into the container.

Step 5: Automate Container Deployment Using Docker Compose

1. Create a docker-compose.yml file:

yaml

```
version: '3'
services:
  web:
    image: nginx
    ports:
      - "80:80"
    volumes:
      - ./nginx.conf:/etc/nginx/nginx.conf
```

2. Run the application using Docker Compose:

bash

```
$ sudo docker-compose up -d
```

o   This will start the Nginx container with the specified configuration.

Summary

In this chapter, we explored **Docker**, **LXD**, and virtualization tools like **KVM** and **VirtualBox**. We covered the installation and usage of Docker, including creating and managing containers, building custom images, and using Docker Compose to automate multi-container applications. We also looked at system containerization with **LXD**, which is more suited for running full Linux distributions in containers.

The real-world example demonstrated how to set up a simple **Nginx web server** inside a Docker container and automate the process using Docker Compose. Virtualization and containers are essential technologies for modern infrastructure, enabling better resource utilization, scalability, and ease of management.

In the next chapter, we will explore advanced system administration topics such as performance profiling, automation, and managing system logs.

CHAPTER 23

MANAGING SERVICES AND DAEMONS

Managing services and daemons is a crucial task for any Linux system administrator. Services (also known as daemons) are background processes that run on the system to provide various functionalities like web servers, databases, or system monitoring. In this chapter, we will explore how to manage services and daemons using the most common service management tools in Linux: **systemd**, **Upstart**, and **init.d**. We will also walk through a real-world example of configuring a service to start on boot.

Managing Services with systemd

systemd is the most widely used system and service manager on modern Linux distributions. It replaces older init systems (like **SysVinit**) and offers powerful tools for managing services and the system as a whole.

1. **Systemd Overview**:
   o **systemd** is responsible for starting and managing system services, handling system initialization

(booting), and providing a unified interface to monitor system status.

- ○ Services are represented by **unit files** in `/etc/systemd/system/` (for custom services) or `/lib/systemd/system/` (for installed services).

2. **Managing Services with systemd**:

   - ○ To start a service:

```bash
$ sudo systemctl start <service_name>
```

  - Example: To start the Nginx service:

```bash
$ sudo systemctl start nginx
```

   - ○ To stop a service:

```bash
$ sudo systemctl stop <service_name>
```

  - Example: To stop Nginx:

```bash
```

```
$ sudo systemctl stop nginx
```

o   To restart a service:

```
bash
```

```
$     sudo     systemctl     restart
<service_name>
```

o   To check the status of a service:

```
bash
```

```
$     sudo     systemctl     status
<service_name>
```

- Example:

```
bash
```

```
$ sudo systemctl status nginx
```

o   To enable a service to start automatically at boot:

```
bash
```

```
$     sudo     systemctl     enable
<service_name>
```

262

o   To disable a service from starting at boot:

bash

```
$    sudo    systemctl    disable
<service_name>
```

o   To check if a service is enabled or disabled:

bash

```
$    sudo    systemctl    is-enabled
<service_name>
```

3. **Viewing Logs with `journalctl`:**

o   `systemd` uses the **journal** to collect and manage logs from services. To view logs for a specific service:

bash

```
$ sudo journalctl -u <service_name>
```

▪   Example:

bash

```
$ sudo journalctl -u nginx
```

4. **Creating Custom Systemd Services:**

263

o To create a custom service, you can create a unit file in /etc/systemd/system/. For example:

```ini
[Unit]
Description=My Custom Service

[Service]
ExecStart=/path/to/my/command

[Install]
WantedBy=multi-user.target
```

o Save the unit file, reload systemd, and enable the service:

```bash
$ sudo systemctl daemon-reload
$ sudo systemctl enable my_custom_service
$ sudo systemctl start my_custom_service
```

Managing Services with Upstart

Upstart was an event-driven system used in older versions of Ubuntu (before 15.04) and some other Linux distributions. Upstart is used to manage system services, similar to **systemd**.

1. **Managing Services with Upstart**:
    - o To start a service with Upstart:

      bash

      ```
      $ sudo start <service_name>
      ```

    - o To stop a service with Upstart:

      bash

      ```
      $ sudo stop <service_name>
      ```

    - o To check the status of a service:

      bash

      ```
      $ sudo status <service_name>
      ```

2. **Service Configuration**:
    - o Upstart configuration files are typically stored in `/etc/init/` and have a `.conf` extension.

265

o To enable a service to start at boot, Upstart automatically uses the **start on** directive in the service configuration file. Example of a basic Upstart configuration:

```ini
description "My Custom Service"
start on runlevel [2345]
stop on runlevel [!2345]

script
    /path/to/my/command
end script
```

Managing Services with init.d

init.d is the traditional service management system used in older Linux distributions, where service scripts are stored in `/etc/init.d/`.

1. **Managing Services with init.d**:
   o To start a service with init.d:

```bash
$ sudo /etc/init.d/<service_name> start
```

266

o   To stop a service with init.d:

```bash

$ sudo /etc/init.d/<service_name> stop
```

o   To restart a service with init.d:

```bash

$ sudo /etc/init.d/<service_name> restart
```

o   To check the status of a service:

```bash

$ sudo /etc/init.d/<service_name> status
```

2. **Enabling Services to Start on Boot**:

o   On Debian-based systems, you can use update-rc.d to enable or disable a service:

```bash

$ sudo update-rc.d <service_name> defaults
```

- o On Red Hat-based systems, you can use `chkconfig`:

bash

```
$ sudo chkconfig <service_name> on
```

Real-World Example: Configuring a Service to Start on Boot

In this real-world example, we will configure the **Nginx** web server to start automatically on boot using **systemd**.

Step 1: Install Nginx

If Nginx is not already installed, you can install it using your package manager.

1. **On Ubuntu/Debian**:

   bash

   ```
   $ sudo apt update
   $ sudo apt install nginx
   ```

2. **On CentOS/RHEL**:

   bash

```
$ sudo yum install nginx
```

Step 2: Start the Nginx Service

Start the Nginx service manually:

bash

```
$ sudo systemctl start nginx
```

Step 3: Enable Nginx to Start on Boot

To configure Nginx to start automatically when the system boots, use the `systemctl enable` command:

bash

```
$ sudo systemctl enable nginx
```

This command creates a symbolic link in the appropriate system directories to ensure Nginx is started during boot.

Step 4: Verify the Service is Enabled

To verify that the Nginx service is enabled and will start on boot, run:

bash

```
$ sudo systemctl is-enabled nginx
```

The output should be:

```
nginx

enabled
```

Step 5: Check the Service Status

To confirm that Nginx is running, check the service status:

```bash
$ sudo systemctl status nginx
```

You should see output indicating that Nginx is active and running.

Step 6: Reboot and Verify

Finally, reboot your system to verify that Nginx starts automatically:

```bash
$ sudo reboot
```

After the system reboots, check if Nginx is running:

```bash
```

```
$ sudo systemctl status nginx
```

If Nginx starts successfully, your configuration is complete.

Summary

In this chapter, we covered how to manage services and daemons in Linux using **systemd**, **Upstart**, and **init.d**. We explored how to start, stop, enable, and disable services with these tools. Additionally, we walked through a real-world example of configuring the **Nginx** web server to start on boot using **systemd**.

systemd is the most widely used service manager on modern Linux systems, but understanding how to work with older systems like **Upstart** and **init.d** is still important, especially when managing legacy systems.

Efficient service management ensures that critical services are available when needed and run with minimal overhead. In the next chapter, we will explore advanced service management techniques, including logging, monitoring, and troubleshooting services.

Part 7

Linux Security

CHAPTER 24

SECURITY BASICS FOR LINUX SYSADMINS

Security is a top priority for system administrators, especially when managing Linux systems that are exposed to the internet. Ensuring that your systems are secure against attacks requires configuring user accounts, file systems, and network services properly. In this chapter, we will cover fundamental security practices for Linux sysadmins, including securing user accounts, file systems, and SSH access. We will also provide a real-world example of securing a web server from common attacks.

Securing User Accounts

User accounts are often the first line of defense in a Linux system. Proper account management is crucial for ensuring that unauthorized users cannot gain access to your system.

1. **Creating Strong Passwords**:
   - o Enforce strong passwords by configuring **Pluggable Authentication Modules (PAM)**. In particular, the `pam_pwquality.so` module can enforce password strength policies.

o Edit `/etc/security/pwquality.conf` to set password policies:

```bash
minlen = 12
minclass = 3
```

o `minlen` enforces a minimum password length, and `minclass` requires a mix of character types (lowercase, uppercase, digits, and special characters).

2. **Using `passwd` to Set Password Expiration**:

o To force users to change their passwords regularly, you can set password expiration policies with the `chage` command:

```bash
$ sudo chage -M 30 username
```

o This command sets the password expiration to 30 days for the specified user.

3. **Locking Inactive Accounts**:

o Disable inactive accounts to prevent unauthorized access. For example, to lock a user account:

```
bash
```

```
$ sudo usermod -L username
```

4. Restricting Root Access:

- o Use the **sudo** mechanism to restrict access to root privileges. Disable direct root login by modifying the /etc/ssh/sshd_config file:

```
bash
```

```
PermitRootLogin no
```

- o Ensure that only authorized users have sudo privileges by editing the /etc/sudoers file using visudo:

```
bash
```

```
$ sudo visudo
```

5. Removing Unused User Accounts:

- o Clean up user accounts that are no longer in use to reduce potential attack vectors:

```
bash
```

```
$ sudo userdel username
```

Securing the File System

The file system is where critical system files and user data are stored. Securing it is essential to prevent unauthorized access and tampering.

1. **Setting Proper File Permissions**:
    o   Use **chmod**, **chown**, and **chgrp** to set the correct permissions on files and directories.
    o   For example, to make a file readable and writable only by the owner:

    bash

    ```
    $ sudo chmod 600 /path/to/file
    ```

2. **Using umask to Set Default Permissions**:
    o   The umask command sets default file creation permissions. For example, to set a default of rw-r--r-- for all newly created files, add the following line to /etc/profile or /etc/bashrc:

    bash

    ```
    umask 022
    ```

3. **Mounting File Systems with `noexec`, `nosuid`, and `nodev`:**

   o Use these mount options to enhance security by preventing the execution of binaries and the use of special device files.

   o For example, to mount a directory with these restrictions:

   bash

   ```
   $ sudo mount -o noexec,nosuid,nodev /mnt
   ```

   o Add this line to `/etc/fstab` for persistent mounting:

   bash

   ```
   /dev/sdb1          /mnt          ext4
   noexec,nosuid,nodev 0 2
   ```

4. **Encrypting Sensitive Data:**

   o Use full disk encryption or specific file encryption for sensitive data. **LUKS** is commonly used for encrypting disks, while tools like **gpg** can be used to encrypt individual files:

   bash

277

```
$ gpg -c /path/to/file
```

5. **Checking for World-Writable Files**:

- o Periodically check for world-writable files, which can be exploited by attackers:

bash

```
$ sudo find / -type f -perm -0002
```

Securing SSH Access

SSH is the most common method for remotely accessing Linux servers. Securing SSH access is essential to prevent unauthorized access and attacks like brute force.

1. **Disabling Password-Based Authentication**:

- o Use **SSH key authentication** and disable password-based login. Edit the /etc/ssh/sshd_config file:

bash

```
PasswordAuthentication no
```

- o Restart the SSH service:

```
bash
```

```
$ sudo systemctl restart sshd
```

2. Using SSH Keys Instead of Passwords:

o Generate an SSH key pair and the public key to the server:

```
bash
```

```
$ ssh-keygen
$ ssh--id user@remote-server
```

3. Limiting SSH Access to Specific IPs:

o To restrict SSH access to specific IP addresses, add the following lines to the /etc/ssh/sshd_config file:

```
bash
```

```
AllowUsers user@192.168.1.100
```

o Restart SSH after making changes:

```
bash
```

```
$ sudo systemctl restart sshd
```

4. Changing the Default SSH Port:

- o Change the default SSH port from 22 to something less predictable:

bash

```
Port 2222
```

- o Make sure to update the firewall rules to allow the new port.

5. **Using Two-Factor Authentication (2FA)**:
   - o For an additional layer of security, enable two-factor authentication for SSH using tools like **Google Authenticator**:

bash

```
$ sudo apt-get install libpam-
google-authenticator
```

   - o Follow the instructions to set up 2FA for SSH.

6. **Fail2Ban to Prevent Brute-Force Attacks**:
   - o Install **Fail2Ban** to monitor SSH logs and block IPs after a certain number of failed login attempts:

bash

```
$ sudo apt install fail2ban
```

280

o Configure it to monitor `/var/log/auth.log` for SSH login attempts and block offending IP addresses.

Real-World Example: Securing a Web Server from Common Attacks

Web servers are common targets for attackers. Securing a web server is critical to protecting your data and services. Let's go through the steps of securing a web server (such as **Nginx** or **Apache**) from common attacks.

Step 1: Install and Configure the Web Server

1. Install the web server (e.g., Nginx or Apache):

bash

```
$ sudo apt install nginx
```

2. Start and enable the web server:

bash

```
$ sudo systemctl start nginx
$ sudo systemctl enable nginx
```

Step 2: Secure Nginx or Apache Configuration

1. **Disable Directory Listing**:

   o In Nginx, ensure directory listing is disabled:

   ```bash
   autoindex off;
   ```

2. **Limit HTTP Methods**:

   o Limit the allowed HTTP methods (e.g., only allow GET and POST):

   ```bash
   limit_except GET POST {
     deny all;
   }
   ```

3. **Hide Server Information**:

   o In Nginx, prevent the web server from revealing its version:

   ```bash
   server_tokens off;
   ```

4. **Implement SSL/TLS**:

o   Use **Let's Encrypt** or another SSL provider to secure web traffic with HTTPS.

o   Install Certbot and configure SSL:

```bash
$ sudo apt install certbot python3-
certbot-nginx
$ sudo certbot --nginx
```

Step 3: Set Up a Web Application Firewall (WAF)

1. Install and configure a WAF, such as **ModSecurity** for Apache or **NAXSI** for Nginx, to detect and block malicious requests.

Step 4: Set Up Rate Limiting

1. In Nginx, enable rate limiting to protect against DoS (Denial of Service) and brute-force attacks:

```bash
limit_req_zone            $binary_remote_addr
zone=one:10m rate=1r/s;
limit_req zone=one burst=5;
```

Step 5: Secure Permissions and Files

1. Set strict file permissions on web content:

```bash
```

```bash
$ sudo chmod 644 /var/www/html/*
$ sudo chmod 755 /var/www/html
```

2. Ensure that the web server user (e.g., `www-data` for Nginx/Apache) only has the minimum necessary permissions.

Step 6: Regularly Update the Web Server

1. Regularly update your web server and associated software to patch known vulnerabilities:

```bash
```

```bash
$ sudo apt update
$ sudo apt upgrade nginx
```

Summary

In this chapter, we explored the basics of securing user accounts, file systems, and SSH access on Linux systems. We covered essential security practices such as enforcing strong passwords, restricting root access, managing file permissions, and using encryption. We also discussed securing SSH access by disabling password authentication, using SSH keys, and implementing two-factor authentication.

The real-world example demonstrated how to secure a web server (Nginx or Apache) by limiting HTTP methods, implementing SSL/TLS encryption, setting up rate limiting, and using a web application firewall. By following these security practices, you can protect your Linux systems from common attacks and ensure their integrity.

In the next chapter, we will dive deeper into advanced security topics such as intrusion detection systems (IDS), security auditing, and monitoring.

CHAPTER 25

ADVANCED SECURITY CONFIGURATIONS

In addition to basic security practices, advanced security configurations provide an extra layer of protection for Linux systems. Tools like **SELinux**, **AppArmor**, and other security modules allow sysadmins to enforce fine-grained access controls and prevent unauthorized access to critical system resources. This chapter will introduce **SELinux**, **AppArmor**, and other security modules, and provide a real-world example of configuring SELinux on a **CentOS** server for enhanced security.

SELinux (Security-Enhanced Linux)

SELinux is a Linux security module that provides an additional layer of security by enforcing access control policies. Unlike traditional discretionary access control (DAC) systems (such as file permissions), SELinux uses mandatory access control (MAC), which restricts the actions that users and processes can perform based on security policies.

1. **Key Concepts in SELinux**:
   - o **Security Context**: Every process and file on an SELinux-enabled system is labeled with a security context that defines its security attributes. The context is made up of a user, role, type, and level (e.g., `system_u:object_r:httpd_t:s0`).
   - o **Policy**: SELinux enforces rules (policies) that determine what actions are allowed on objects. These policies are predefined and can be customized.
   - o **Modes**:
     - **Enforcing**: SELinux policy is enforced, and violations are blocked.
     - **Permissive**: SELinux policy is not enforced, but violations are logged.
     - **Disabled**: SELinux is turned off completely.

2. **Checking SELinux Status**:
   - o To check the current status of SELinux on a system:

```bash
$ getenforce
```

- This will return one of the following values: `Enforcing`, `Permissive`, or `Disabled`.
  - To get detailed information about SELinux configuration:

```bash
$ sestatus
```

3. **Changing SELinux Modes**:
   - To temporarily set SELinux to **permissive** mode (for troubleshooting):

```bash
$ sudo setenforce 0
```

   - To set SELinux back to **enforcing** mode:

```bash
$ sudo setenforce 1
```

4. **Configuring SELinux**:
   - SELinux settings are configured in the `/etc/selinux/config` file. You can modify the mode permanently by editing this file:

288

```
bash
```

```
$ sudo nano /etc/selinux/config
```

- Set `SELINUX=enforcing` to enable enforcing mode, `SELINUX=permissive` for permissive mode, or `SELINUX=disabled` to disable SELinux.

5. **SELinux File Contexts**:

   o Files and directories are labeled with security contexts that define their allowed interactions. You can check a file's context using `ls -Z`:

   ```
   bash
   ```

   ```
   $ ls -Z /path/to/file
   ```

   o To change the security context of a file, use `chcon`:

   ```
   bash
   ```

   ```
   $ sudo chcon -t httpd_sys_content_t
   /var/www/html/index.html
   ```

6. **SELinux Troubleshooting**:

- o If SELinux is blocking certain actions, you can view the logs in `/var/log/audit/audit.log` for details.
- o Use the `ausearch` tool to search for SELinux audit logs:

bash

```
$ sudo ausearch -m avc -ts recent
```

- o **Audit2Allow** can help generate SELinux policy rules to allow specific actions:

bash

```
$ sudo audit2allow -a
```

AppArmor

AppArmor (Application Armor) is another Linux security module that works by enforcing security policies that restrict the actions that programs can perform based on the files they can access and the capabilities they can use. Unlike SELinux, which uses a detailed policy language, AppArmor policies are simpler and focused on restricting access for individual applications.

1. **Installing and Managing AppArmor**:

   o To install AppArmor on a Debian/Ubuntu-based system:

   ```bash
   $ sudo apt install apparmor apparmor-utils
   ```

   o To check the status of AppArmor:

   ```bash
   $ sudo aa-status
   ```

2. **Enabling and Disabling AppArmor Profiles**:

   o To enable a profile for an application:

   ```bash
   $ sudo aa-enforce /etc/apparmor.d/usr.bin.nginx
   ```

   o To disable a profile for troubleshooting:

   ```bash
   $ sudo aa-disable /etc/apparmor.d/usr.bin.nginx
   ```

291

3. **AppArmor Profiles**:

   o AppArmor profiles are stored in `/etc/apparmor.d/`. You can edit or create custom profiles for applications by modifying these files.

   o Example: Editing the AppArmor profile for Nginx:

   bash

   ```
   $          sudo          nano
   /etc/apparmor.d/usr.bin.nginx
   ```

   o After editing, reload the profile:

   bash

   ```
   $    sudo    apparmor_parser    -r
   /etc/apparmor.d/usr.bin.nginx
   ```

4. **AppArmor Logs**:

   o AppArmor logs events to `/var/log/syslog` or `/var/log/audit/audit.log`. Check the logs for denied actions by AppArmor profiles.

5. **AppArmor vs SELinux**:

   o AppArmor is generally easier to configure and less intrusive compared to SELinux, but SELinux provides more fine-grained security controls. Your choice between AppArmor and SELinux depends on your needs and the distribution you are using.

Other Linux Security Modules

1. **TOMOYO Linux**:
   - **TOMOYO** is another security module that focuses on mandatory access control, but it uses a simpler configuration system compared to SELinux and AppArmor. It provides fine-grained access control based on the behavior of applications.

2. **Linux Security Modules (LSM)**:
   - **LSM** is a framework for security modules in Linux, allowing multiple modules to be used at the same time (e.g., SELinux, AppArmor, TOMOYO). You can see which security modules are enabled on your system by checking the kernel configuration:

   bash

   ```
   $ sudo cat /boot/config-$(uname -r)
   | grep CONFIG_SECURITY
   ```

Real-World Example: Configuring SELinux on a CentOS Server for Enhanced Security

In this example, we will configure **SELinux** on a **CentOS** server to enforce a security policy and restrict the actions of specific services.

Step 1: Check SELinux Status

1. First, check the current status of SELinux on the CentOS server:

    bash

    ```
    $ getenforce
    ```

    If it returns `Disabled`, you need to enable SELinux in the configuration file.

Step 2: Enable SELinux

1. Open the SELinux configuration file for editing:

    bash

    ```
    $ sudo nano /etc/selinux/config
    ```

2. Set **SELINUX** to `enforcing` mode:

```ini
ini
```

```
SELINUX=enforcing
```

3. Save the file and exit the editor.
4. Reboot the system to apply the changes:

```bash
bash
```

```
$ sudo reboot
```

Step 3: Verify SELinux Is Enabled

After the system has rebooted, check the status again to ensure SELinux is now enabled:

```bash
bash
```

```
$ getenforce
```

It should return `Enforcing`.

Step 4: Set File Contexts

If you are running a web server (e.g., Nginx or Apache), you may need to adjust the file contexts for web content directories.

1. Set the proper SELinux context for the Nginx web directory:

bash

```
$ sudo chcon -t httpd_sys_content_t /var/www/html -R
```

2. If using Apache, use:

bash

```
$ sudo chcon -t httpd_sys_content_t /var/www/html -R
```

Step 5: Troubleshooting with Audit Logs

1. If SELinux blocks a legitimate action, you can find the denial message in the audit log:

bash

```
$ sudo cat /var/log/audit/audit.log | grep AVC
```

2. Use **audit2allow** to generate a policy module to allow the action:

bash

```
$ sudo ausearch -c 'httpd' --raw |
audit2allow -M my-httpd-policy
$ sudo semodule -i my-httpd-policy.pp
```

Step 6: Use SELinux for Web Server Security

Now, with SELinux enabled and configured, the web server is more secure. SELinux enforces access control, ensuring that processes can only access the files and resources they need, preventing exploitation in the event of a vulnerability.

Summary

In this chapter, we explored advanced security configurations in Linux, focusing on **SELinux** and **AppArmor**. We covered how to enable and configure SELinux to enforce a security policy and manage file contexts for web servers. We also introduced other Linux security modules, such as **TOMOYO**, and provided a comparison between SELinux and AppArmor.

By utilizing SELinux and AppArmor, you can create more secure systems by enforcing strict access control policies and minimizing the risk of security breaches. In the next chapter, we will dive deeper into intrusion detection systems, security auditing, and monitoring techniques to ensure your Linux systems remain secure.

CHAPTER 26

AUDITING AND COMPLIANCE

Auditing and ensuring compliance are critical tasks for maintaining the security and integrity of Linux systems. Proper auditing helps track system activity, detect potential security breaches, and meet regulatory requirements. In this chapter, we will explore tools and strategies for auditing Linux systems for security and compliance, focusing on **auditd** and **syslog**. We will also provide a real-world example of ensuring **GDPR** compliance on a Linux web server.

Auditing Linux Systems with auditd

auditd (Audit Daemon) is a powerful tool used to monitor and log system activities in Linux. It enables system administrators to record events such as file access, system calls, and security-related activities. This is particularly useful for tracking potential breaches and meeting compliance requirements, such as those mandated by GDPR, HIPAA, or PCI-DSS.

1. **Installing and Configuring auditd**:

- o On most Linux distributions, you can install **auditd** using the package manager:
  - On Ubuntu/Debian:

  ```bash
  $ sudo apt install auditd
  ```

  - On CentOS/RHEL:

  ```bash
  $ sudo yum install audit
  ```

2. **Starting and Enabling auditd**:
   - o Start the audit daemon:

   ```bash
   $ sudo systemctl start auditd
   ```

   - o Enable it to start on boot:

   ```bash
   $ sudo systemctl enable auditd
   ```

3. **Configuring auditd**:
   - o The configuration file for **auditd** is located at `/etc/audit/auditd.conf`. You can adjust

300

settings like the log file location, maximum log file size, and log rotation policies.

o   Example:

```bash
```

```
$ sudo nano /etc/audit/auditd.conf
```

o   Set parameters such as:

- **max_log_file**: Maximum size of log files.
- **max_log_file_action**: Action to take when the log file reaches the max size (e.g., `rotate`).
- **log_format**: Specify the format of the log file (e.g., `ENRICHED`).

4. **Creating Audit Rules**:

o   Audit rules define what activities should be logged. These rules are stored in `/etc/audit/rules.d/` or `/etc/audit/audit.rules`.

o   Example: Log all file accesses in the `/etc` directory:

```bash
```

```
$ sudo auditctl -w /etc -p war -k
etc_access
```

- -w: Watch a file or directory.
- -p war: Log write, attribute change, and read actions.
- -k etc_access: Assign a key to identify the rule in logs.

o To persist the rule after reboot, add it to /etc/audit/rules.d/audit.rules.

5. **Viewing Audit Logs**:

o The logs are stored in /var/log/audit/audit.log. You can use ausearch to query the logs for specific events:

bash

```
$ sudo ausearch -k etc_access
```

o To analyze the logs in more detail:

bash

```
$ sudo aureport
```

6. **Generating Reports**:

o The **aureport** command generates summarized reports based on audit logs, such as a summary of all file accesses or user activities:

bash

```
$ sudo aureport -f
```

7. **Monitoring Specific Activities**:

o To audit successful and failed login attempts:

bash

```
$ sudo auditctl -w /var/log/secure -
p wa -k login_activity
```

Using syslog for Auditing and Logging

syslog is a standard for logging system messages. It allows different services and applications to write logs to a central log file or send them to a logging server. On Linux, **rsyslog** is commonly used as the syslog daemon.

1. **Configuring rsyslog**:

o The main configuration file for **rsyslog** is /etc/rsyslog.conf. You can configure it to store logs in specific files, send logs to remote servers, or filter logs based on their severity.

o Example configuration to store all logs in `/var/log/all.log`:

bash

```
*.* /var/log/all.log
```

2. Viewing Syslog Logs:

o The default system log file is `/var/log/syslog`. You can view the logs using `cat`, `less`, or `tail`:

bash

```
$ tail -f /var/log/syslog
```

3. Remote Logging with rsyslog:

o To send logs to a remote server, add the following to `/etc/rsyslog.conf`:

bash

```
*.* @remote-server-ip:514
```

4. Log Rotation:

- o Logs can grow rapidly, so log rotation is necessary to manage their size. The logrotate tool is used to rotate logs and compress old log files.
- o The configuration files for **logrotate** are located in `/etc/logrotate.conf` and `/etc/logrotate.d/`.

Real-World Example: Ensuring GDPR Compliance on a Linux Web Server

The **General Data Protection Regulation (GDPR)** mandates that organizations protect the personal data and privacy of EU citizens. Ensuring GDPR compliance on a Linux web server involves auditing and monitoring the storage and access of personal data.

Step 1: Review Data Collection Practices

1. **Identify Personal Data**:
   - o Personal data includes any information that can be used to identify an individual (e.g., names, email addresses, IP addresses).
   - o On a web server, this may include data collected via form submissions, cookies, and login information.

2. **Monitor Data Access**:

   o Use **auditd** to track access to sensitive data files or directories. For example, if user data is stored in `/var/www/data`, create a rule to log access to that directory:

   bash

   ```
   $ sudo auditctl -w /var/www/data -p war -k personal_data_access
   ```

   Step 2: Enable Logging for Data Access

1. **Set Up Syslog for Security Audits**:

   o Ensure that all security-related events (e.g., user logins, file access, failed login attempts) are logged in `/var/log/syslog` or `/var/log/auth.log`.

   o For example, configure **rsyslog** to log authentication events:

   bash

   ```
   auth,authpriv.* /var/log/auth.log
   ```

2. **Use Fail2Ban to Block Malicious IPs**:

o Install **Fail2Ban** to protect against brute-force attacks and ensure unauthorized users cannot gain access to sensitive personal data.

bash

```
$ sudo apt install fail2ban
```

o Configure Fail2Ban to monitor `/var/log/auth.log` for failed login attempts and ban IPs after a defined number of failed attempts.

Step 3: Ensure Data Encryption

1. **Encrypt Sensitive Data**:
   o Ensure that sensitive data (such as personal information) is encrypted, both in transit (via SSL/TLS) and at rest (via disk encryption).
   o For web traffic, use **Let's Encrypt** to install an SSL certificate:

bash

```
$ sudo certbot --nginx
```

o For sensitive files, use **gpg** to encrypt them:

307

```
bash
```

```
$ gpg -c /path/to/sensitive_data.txt
```

Step 4: Regular Audits and Reports

1. **Audit Logs for Compliance**:

    o   Regularly audit logs to ensure that data access
        policies are being followed. For example, use
        ausearch to search for unauthorized access:

    ```
    bash
    ```

    ```
    $       sudo        ausearch       -k
    personal_data_access
    ```

2. **Generate Regular Reports**:

    o   Use `aureport` to generate audit reports that
        track who accessed what data, when, and why.
        These reports are important for compliance
        documentation.

    ```
    bash
    ```

    ```
    $ sudo aureport -f -i
    ```

Step 5: Secure Data Storage and Deletion

1. **Data Retention and Deletion**:

- o Set up data retention policies to ensure that personal data is not kept longer than necessary. Ensure that the data is securely deleted when no longer required.
- o For secure file deletion, use tools like `shred` or `wipe`:

bash

```
$ sudo shred -u /path/to/file
```

Summary

In this chapter, we explored tools and techniques for auditing Linux systems for security and compliance, focusing on **auditd** and **syslog**. We discussed how to monitor system activities, track access to sensitive data, and ensure compliance with standards like **GDPR**.

The real-world example demonstrated how to ensure GDPR compliance on a Linux web server by auditing data access, logging security events, encrypting sensitive data, and performing regular audits. By following these practices, sysadmins can help ensure that their systems meet the necessary security and compliance requirements.

In the next chapter, we will dive into more advanced security configurations, including intrusion detection systems (IDS), advanced firewall configurations, and network monitoring.

www.ingramcontent.com/pod-product-compliance
Lightning Source LLC
LaVergne TN
LVHW022335060326
832902LV00022B/4051